Great
Mysteries
of History

Kenneth B. Platnick

DORSET PRESS
New York

First published by David & Charles (Publishers) Ltd., 1972

This edition published by Dorset Press,
a division of Marboro Books Corporation,
by arrangement with
David & Charles (Publishers) Ltd.
1987 Dorset Press

ISBN 0-88029-157-5

Printed in the United States of America

M 9 8

Contents

Fact or Fantasy?

Preface

IS FACT REALLY stranger than fiction?

You can read James Bond thrillers and marvel at the intricacies of plot, technology, and daring. You can thrill to the old-fashioned prowess of detectives like Sam Spade and Mike Shayne. You can struggle along with the ageless Ellery Queen and Perry Mason as they solve one mystery after another in a world of murder and mayhem. And the clues fall cleverly into place at the end.

The unsolved mysteries of history have no such endings. But they have real beginnings. Maybe that's what makes them seem so much stranger. Certainly it makes them all the more exciting.

Everyone, of course, has his own selection of "favorites" among these unsolved mysteries. Not all of them are represented here. This collection is necessarily limited by the twin criteria of mysteriousness and greatness implicit in the title.

The very nature of mystery accounts for the fact that no attempt has been made to offer solutions. At best, it would be risky scholarship; at worst, presumptuous. The cases remain unsolved.

To qualify as "great," however, the mysteries must not only be unsolved. They must, it seems, involve persons celebrated in the course of history or events of some real meaning for history.

Amy Robsart and Sir Edmund Berry Godfrey, for example, were anything but celebrities in their time. Neither has succeeded to fame in the centuries since. But each died under circumstances so suspect as to threaten the very security of the English crown and the uneasy head thereof.

With the lost dauphin and the Man in the Iron Mask, it's quite another story. Each had a certain claim to historical importance in his own right. But the greatness of the mysteries surrounding them today derives mainly from the continuing strength of popular interest. These are romantic mysteries, derived from the days of Dumas and de Vigny.

Romance, too, is at the heart of the stories of Anastasia

and Alexander I. In fairness, though, it must be noted that any version of the latter, however unromantic, would still merit considerable attention. When a czar walks out on his czardom, that's news. When he is said to have disappeared thereafter to live the life of a hermit in Siberia, even a writer like Dumas seems strangely unimaginative.

Romance borders on fantasy in the tales of lost continents, of lost colonies and cultures. Their mystery is the essence of history.

In our own time, the disappearance of Judge Crater has become a classic of its genre, the name of Jack the Ripper a synonym for misguided misogynists. And the mere possibility that such creatures as the Abominable Snowman and the Loch Ness monster might be real provides the stuff of which pure fiction is made.

*   *

As historical mysteries go, the death of Dag Hammarskjold is still young. But it ages quickly. Too much evidence was ignored at the time of the official investigations. Too much was hidden. With the passing of each year, the facts of the case are buried deeper. In time, they may be lost. For, if there is any recurring theme among these chapters, it is perhaps that history is so easily duped by the willful, often official, concealment of truth. Indifference, evasion, secrecy—these are the breeding grounds of mystery. And even the stubbornness of preconceived notions has hampered investigators in their search for the truth. Hence, the lost clues in such diverse cases as those of Godfrey, the Ripper, and Amy Robsart; the missed opportunities to confirm or deny recognition of Anastasia and the French dauphin, Louis XVII.

Meanwhile, other mysteries take shape around us. Nagging doubts about the report of the 1964 Warren Commission may leave open many channels of inquiry into the murder of

John F. Kennedy. The continued sightings of unidentified flying objects (UFO's) suggest more strongly than ever the surveillance of the earth by visitors from other planets, just as newly discovered radio signals, or pulsars, lend credence to the belief that there may be intelligent life on stars at the very edge of the Milky Way.

Let us hope that no action (or inaction) will be permitted today that may deprive future generations of the means of getting at the truth of these and other matters.

* *

A friend calls me a "mystorian." It's an appropriate term. For it reflects at once the unity of those criteria which have underlain my work.

Fortunately, I have not quite had to bear the entire burden of that work alone. I have had considerable help: from James Rietmulder of Stackpole Books and A. A. Hoehling of the Army Times Publishing Company, who conceived and directed the project; from John Schaffner, a gently prodding literary agent who offered sound professional guidance in the course of its completion; from Marilyn and Edna Platnick, wife and mother, respectively, who devoted long hours to research for several of the book's chapters; from Edna Shamo and Yola Schlosser, who kindly translated key passages from foreign-language sources; from Anne DeCapua and Barbara Gilchrist, who assisted ably in picture research and typing; and from the large number of friends who took interest enough in my work to propose and study other subjects that might be included.

Many of those suggestions came close.

There are the polar mysteries—the lost Franklin expedition, the mysterious death of the Swedish airman Andree, the disappearance of the Norwegian explorer Amundsen. There are mysteries surrounding the sinking of such mighty vessels as the *Maine,* the *Titanic,* and the *Lusitania,* as well as the explosion of the dirigible *Hindenburg*. There are the giant heads of Easter Island and the wondrous treasures of Angkor Wat.

The disappearance of Ambrose Bierce in the hills of Mexico and the curiously underinvestigated murder of Sir Harry Oakes in the Bahamas are both favorite topics among amateur criminologists.

In some cases, real historical significance seemed lacking. In others, the element of mystery was dissipated as research got under way. Credible guesses can be made, for instance, concerning the unhappy fate of Amelia Earhart, who in 1937 disappeared on the last leg of a round-the-world flight. Causes of death can be surmised in the oft-labeled "mysteries" of U.S. President Warren G. Harding and Russian Premier Joseph Stalin.

The reader may differ with some results of this selection. Perhaps it's only natural. But one hopes that he will get past these differences quickly enough to enjoy the stories themselves. Perhaps he will want to delve further into one of these himself and seek the key to its solution. A set of reading notes has, therefore, been provided to help show the way.

Dag Hammarskjold reviewing U.N. troops in the Congo.—*Photograph courtesy Reportagebild, Stockholm*

NAKED AGAINST THE NIGHT

the
mysterious
death
of
Dag Hammarskjold ...

Standing naked
Where they have placed me,
Nailed to the target
By their first arrows.

Again a bow is drawn,
Again an arrow flies,
—and misses.
Are they pretending?
Did a hand shake,
Or was it the wind?

What have I to fear?
If their arrows hit,
If their arrows kill,
What is there in that
To cry about?

Others have gone before,
Others will follow.

1961

AFRICA SLEPT. The jungle night was still and black. Only the slightest breeze rippled through the tall grass of the countryside.

Then, suddenly, at a quarter past twelve, not ten miles west of Ndola airport, a big DC-6B airliner fell from the skies and crashed in blazing wreckage.

This was the *Albertina*. The treetops ripped away her left wing as she struck. Yet, on she rode, shakily and with a terrible speed, cutting a wide swath of devastation along her wooded path.

Those who were not instantly killed by the impact died soon enough in its fiery aftermath.

Only two aboard survived the moment of disaster: the Secretary General of the United Nations, Dag Hammarskjold, and an aide. Hammarskjold himself, thrown safely clear of the crash site, was left to linger in the still of night and perhaps to pray for help. The other crawled some distance, then collapsed.

At length, a pair of native men approached, looking cautiously about them all the while. But they offered no help. They had come only for looting. One of them espied a small machine that looked much like a typewriter still in working order. It would be of considerable value to them in the market place. So they took it with them and were quickly gone.

Now all was still once more, and hopeless. Straining, Hammarskjold clutched at the dead brown leaves on the ground and held them in the fist of his left hand. Then, he died.

> The moon was caught in the branches:
> Bound by its vow,
> My heart was heavy.
>
> Naked against the night
> The trees slept. "Nevertheless,
> Not as I will. . . ."

> The burden remained mine:
> They could not hear my call,
> And all was silence. . . .

In life a poet and scholar as well as a statesman, Dag Hjalmar Agne Carl Hammarskjold was a mystery in his own time. His poetry and private correspondence reflected a constant preoccupation—some called it obsession—with the image of himself on Calvary: "naked against the night" and "nailed to the target."

He was the intellectual of the international set. And few pretended to understand him—the way he went about agreeing with those who spoke against him, the way he insisted on negotiating important policy from a position of weakness rather than from one of strength. But few as well denied the success of his accomplishments. By the age of thirty-one, he had become the youngest man ever to serve as Sweden's undersecretary of finance. Ten years later, he entered the foreign ministry, rising to cabinet rank as deputy minister.

At forty-six, he was appointed chairman of his country's delegation to the United Nations. The next year, he was elected Secretary General of the U.N. General Assembly, a post to which he was reelected for a second five-year term in 1957.

He took on the job with the zeal of religious mission. To him that world organization was more than a forum among men. It was even more than a mediator of international differences. Ideally, it was the first stage in the developing structure of a truly united body of nations. And his own role, he felt, required a highly personal involvement in those disputes which threatened to disrupt it.

In reality, though, he was more like a man trying to put a stop to an endless succession of vicious dogfights. He was attacked from all sides. The British condemned him for his intervention in the Suez affair. The Russians denounced him for his investigation of the Hungarian uprising. The French publicly insulted him for his role in the Bizerte episode during their war with Algeria.

But it was in the Congo that Hammarskjold's leadership was put to its severest test. There the crisis was not easily discerned. Instead, it comprised a complicated and often confusing power struggle, one in which nearly all the larger nations of the world eventually had a hand. "It isn't even anarchy!" the Secretary General once exclaimed. For, within seven months of its independence, there were no fewer than three "governments" running this former Belgian colony simultaneously.

Two of these Hammarskjold merged. It took months of skillful, long-distance diplomacy—not to mention a "U.N. presence" of 20,000 troops—but, by mid-1961, a central government had been established in Leopoldville. The greater challenge, however, remained to the southeast, where the red-and-green flag of secessionist Katanga Province flaunted its defiance of the new regime.

President Moise Tshombe's 10,000-man army was not the largest in the Congo. But it did enjoy the substantial support of Belgian mining interests located in that copper-rich region. Belgian money bought the army's loyalty. Belgian officers trained it. And Belgian arsenals supplied it with the most modern and efficient weaponry—everything from rifles and bayonets to bazookas and triple-barreled rocket projectors.

All told, it was an effective force in repelling the ground assault of United Nations troops supporting the central government. And its one-man air force had the U.N. distinctly outnumbered overhead.

Hammarskjold, who had been calling the signals for intervention from his headquarters in New York, now made up his mind to negotiate a settlement in person. And an invitation to visit Leopoldville in September of 1961 provided him with the necessary stepping-stone to that goal.

He arrived in the African capital on September 13, less than a week before the opening of the seventeenth session of the General Assembly in New York. The most pressing problem on the agenda of that world body would be to resolve the crisis in the Congo. Hammarskjold hoped to return to the delegates with a secure peace already in hand.

Secretly, he made his bid. His aides carried the message to Tshombe that the Secretary General was prepared to meet with him to discuss an immediate cease-fire. The Katangan could pick the time and place. All Hammarskjold was asking was the chance to talk things over, statesman to statesman.

Tshombe gladly said yes. He reveled in this seeming recognition of his own importance. And a rendezvous was duly set for the next day in the Northern Rhodesian town of Ndola, just across the southern border of Katanga Province.

This worried many of Hammarskjold's staff. Tshombe, they argued, was not to be trusted anywhere he could not be closely watched—least of all in his own backyard. It was widely suspected that this rebel premier had already solved his political differences with at least one man, ex-Premier Patrice Lumumba, by the simple expedient of having him murdered.

Despite the risks, the Secretary General made his plans for the mission. This was Sunday, September 17, the thirteenth anniversary of the assassination of the Swedish Count Folke Bernadotte, a United Nations mediator, in Jerusalem. Late that afternoon, he boarded the *Albertina* for Ndola. At his side, Sture Linner, a close friend and colleague, stood briefly chatting with him while they waited.

The six-man crew took their posts, checking again the panel of instruments and the controls. And the other passengers, eight men and a woman of the Secretary General's staff, strapped themselves for take-off. An all-clear signal was relayed from the ground.

Hammarskjold rose and shook Linner's hand.

"Adjo," he whispered. It was a Swedish farewell.

Outside, the blazing sun hung low over the distant Congo bushland. Soon it would be gone, and they would become invisible in the moonless night that followed. Or so they hoped. For the terror of that flight was its constant threat of attack by a single foe: the notorious *Lone Ranger*. This was a Fouga Magister jet fighter that had just spent the week raiding U.N. army outposts one after another in the cities and jungle clearings. That very morning, in fact, it had twice attacked the air base at Kamina, trying to destroy first the control tower and then the transport planes on the ground. Now the commander of that army was himself an airborne target over a hostile region. And there seemed good reason to fear the *Lone Ranger* would strike again.

Every precaution had been taken, therefore, to ensure the safety and secrecy of the Secretary General's special mission. There was no official communication of the flight. Radio contact was restricted. And the flight plan filed by the captain was falsified to disguise the plane's true destination. The very route they chose was so roundabout that it nearly doubled the distance of their trip. Roughly, it was like flying from New York to Chicago by way of Nashville, Tennessee. However, all the security measures thus imposed proved no match for a journalist's persistence. And, within minutes of take-off, every newsman in Leopoldville had somehow learned that the Secretary General had departed, that he planned to land in Ndola, and that the purpose of the flight was to engage in conference with Tshombe.

Reporters flocked to the Rhodesian airfield some 900 miles away to await the plane's arrival. While they waited, they wrote. And when, at last, a craft with U.N. markings made its descent, they had the front-page story ready:

NDOLA, Northern Rhodesia, Monday, Sept. 18—Secretary General Dag Hammarskjold and Moise Tshombe,

President of Katanga Province, met on neutral ground today to discuss a cease-fire.

The United Nations chief and Mr. Tshombe first met briefly at Ndola airport last night after they flew to Northern Rhodesia separately. They then drove to the village of Kitwe, thirty miles northwest of this frontier town, for what informants described as a crucial meeting. . . .

Also present at the talks were Lord Alport, British High Commissioner in the Federation of Rhodesia and Nyasaland, and a representative of the Northern Rhodesian Government.

It was an interesting story, informative to the least detail. Only it was dead wrong.

The Secretary General's chartered plane never landed on the night of September 17 at all. But the British Under Secretary for Foreign Affairs, Lord Lansdowne, did arrive in the early evening aboard a United Nations DC-4—the very plane, in fact, on which Hammarskjold had been expected to travel. It was he whom the reporters—from their distant posts behind a police cordon—mistook for Hammarskjold. And it was he who conferred briefly with Tshombe, though only to make preparations for the "crucial meeting." Rhodesia, after all, was still British territory. And the British wanted to make a good impression.

President Tshombe did drive off to Kitwe, as news reports indicated. However, he did not leave for any diplomatic purpose but simply because he was tired of waiting. Indeed, after an interval of some four hours there, he had grown quite impatient with many of the finer points of diplomacy. If Hammarskjold's business were so important, Hammarskjold could come to him.

Lansdowne himself stayed on an hour and a half longer. Although he had previously agreed to depart Ndola before the Secretary General arrived, he made no move to do so until the *Albertina* was in plain sight. Possibly he had had some grim forebodings of his own about that flight.

The *Albertina*'s radio silence was first broken some four hours after take-off, and that was because Hammarskjold wanted to know if Lansdowne had arrived in Ndola. Now Lansdowne, having just taken off from Ndola airport after the *Albertina* had reported in to receive instructions for an instrument landing, asked his pilot to make contact with the *Albertina*. There was no answer.

Just half an hour before Lansdowne's departure, the *Albertina* flew directly over the airfield for a regular procedure turn. It had not been heard from since.

The lack of communication deeply concerned the British envoy. But it did not seem to bother the Rhodesians at all. Lord Alport deduced that Hammarskjold had, for some reason, changed his mind about landing and gone off to another port for the night—perhaps even back to Leopoldville. There was no longer any reason for him to wait there. He said goodnight to the airport manager and left.

The manager, meanwhile, decided that there was little more for him to do. After all, the High Commissioner himself had assured him there was no cause for concern. Routinely, he transmitted an INCERFA (Uncertain Phase) signal for the overdue plane, then returned to his hotel in Ndola to sleep. A short time later, the air-traffic controller closed the tower for the night; and he, too, went home.

Thus there was only a communicator on duty when a police report came in regarding a mysterious flash in the sky. An assistant inspector had witnessed the flash just west of Ndola at about 12:20 A.M. on Monday, September 18. Moreover, he had seen a plane flying in that direction only minutes earlier. But it had disappeared from view.

The communicator sent two police officers to the airport manager's hotel with the story. There the sleepy official thanked them but explained that nothing could be done about it until daybreak, anyway. So, he went calmly back to bed.

Others, though, did not sleep so easily. In all, seven persons later testified that they had actually seen two planes flying overhead shortly after midnight. One of them, a charcoal burner in the vicinity, noted that a small aircraft seemed to be pursuing a larger one when, suddenly, the larger plane fell to the ground. The other circled once, he said, and then flew off in the direction of Kitwe.

The sun rose that morning at 5:58. Yet, it was nearly an hour later when the Rhodesian aviation authorities bothered to issue a DETRESFA (Distress Phase) signal for a plane that was already seven hours late. And it was three hours after that before any search was begun for the missing craft.

At 3:10 P.M., the wreckage of the *Albertina* was finally sighted. Only then did local officials swing into action. In fact, they were affected with an efficiency so zealous it bordered on the gruesome. No detail of the crash site was too insignificant to be recorded.

Investigators carefully mapped out the area, depicting the position of each corpse and every stray piece of the plane's wreckage. They raked the ground for coins and other small items of personal property that might have belonged to the victims. They even measured the height of nearby anthills— just for the record.

But nothing was found to pinpoint the cause of the tragedy. They could guess only how it had *not* happened. The tree-tops were not scorched, so the plane had probably not been afire before it crashed. There were no parts of the plane located outside the crash site, so the plane was probably intact at the time it struck.

Only one man survived Hammarskjold after the crash. That was Sergeant Harold M. Julien, a security officer with U.N. forces in the Congo. Five days later, he, too, succumbed.

Julien had been badly burned in the crash. He sustained injuries of the skull and body and suffered further from exposure and sunburn during the long interval before his rescue. Probably, doctors agreed, he could have been saved if rescued sooner; and the world would have had the answer to many a question surrounding this mysterious "accident."

As it was, all this former U.S. marine was ever able to contribute were the often-incoherent phrases of his delirium. He mumbled about things like sparks in the sky and explosions and "Mr. Hammarskjold said, 'Go back.'" A prolonged interrogation by Senior Inspector Allen of the Northern Rhodesian Police was later recorded in full-sentence dialogue:

> Allen: The last we heard from you you were over Ndola runway. What happened?
> Julien: It blew up.
> Allen: Was this over the runway?
> Julien: Yes.
> Allen: What happened then?
> Julien: There was great speed. Great speed.
> Allen: What happened then?
> Julien: Then there was the crash.
> Allen: What happened then?
> Julien: There were lots of little explosions all around.

Did this mean that the *Albertina* was fired on as it prepared to land? Or that a bomb exploded within the craft? Or that the plane had been otherwise sabotaged? Or were these merely the ravings of a delirious man? The attendant surgeon pointed to the possibility of retrograde amnesia and urged inquirers not to take the testimony too seriously.

But the world needed no Julien to prompt such questions. Rumors were rampant—some blaming a stowaway hijacker for the crash, others alleging that the crash was actually staged after Hammarskjold had been murdered in cold blood by Tshombe's guards. Most, however, disavowed any special knowledge of the circumstances. They only knew that a murderous deed had been done.

"Dag Hammarskjold," said Harry S. Truman, former President of the United States, "was on the point of getting something done when they killed him." He paused and stared at the reporters. "Notice that I said, 'When they killed him.'"

And even Andrew Cordier, executive assistant to the late Secretary General, confided to U.N. television producer Emery Kelen, "If I had had to shoot down Hammarskjold's plane I should have done it exactly where it was done."

Transair, the Swedish airline that had leased the *Albertina*, sent its chief engineer to the scene. There he found that several of the victims' bodies were literally riddled with bullets when they were discovered. They might, he suggested, have been shot in the course of an attack on the plane. Moreover, there was a hole in the window frame on the right side of the cockpit that looked very much like a bullet hole.

Skepticism prevailed. Uncertainty clouded public opinion around the world. Could the Federation's own investigators be relied upon to make an objective study when their territory's very reputation was at stake? Might they not be more anxious to "prove" that no such assassination had occurred in Rhodesia than they would be to examine the facts alone?

And, indeed, the Rhodesian commission of inquiry wasted little time in absolving the Federation of any responsibility. Its official verdict—the only one available after four weeks of discounting every other possibility—was "pilot error." The operating crew, the investigators reported, had simply misread or ignored the altimeters and allowed the plane to fly at a dangerously low level. Airport and government personnel, however, had acted with laudable care and efficiency in arranging for the landing of the *Albertina* and, later, for the discovery of the missing plane.

There was no question of attack, the commission held. None of the bullets found in the bodies bore any trace of having passed through a gun barrel, and all matched the caliber of weapons found in the wreckage. Obviously, the ammunition had exploded in the fire that followed the crash. Futhermore, a spectrographic analysis of the hole in the cockpit showed no sign of bullet penetration.

"At the outset," the commissioners stated, "we would say that no reason was suggested, and we cannot think of one, why anyone who might have been able to attack this aircraft from the air should ever have wanted to attack it as it carried Mr. Hammarskjold on the mission he was then undertaking."

From the outset, however, many such motives and suspects were suggested in all corners of the world. The Secretary General had many enemies, British and Belgian among them. The Katangan president had friends, notably Rhodesian and Belgian. And on the day Hammarskjold's death was announced in the Soviet Union, Radio Moscow commented coolly that "the time is ripe for structural changes."

Tshombe himself was far from being above suspicion at the time, although in retrospect he seems to have stood to gain little by the assassination. The Secretary General was playing it his way. Their negotiations might have borne sweet fruits for them both.

Not so, however, for Godefroid Munongo, Tshombe's Minister of the Interior. Munongo was the Katangan "heavy" in the eyes of the world—the man reported to have actually carried out the murder of Patrice Lumumba and to have terrorized all opposition. He thrived on the violent disorder of the Congo.

Munongo's officers were not only Belgian but French as well—Algerian French at that. "They were, and are, fascists," wrote Conor Cruise O'Brien, Hammarskjold's man in Katanga, "and they had scores other than the Congo to settle with Hammarskjold: Algeria, Suez, Tunisia. . . . There is no doubt that they were experienced in political assassination and that they would have regarded the murder of Hammarskjold as a virtuous act."

Within the circle of confusion that described authority throughout the Congo, it may well have been Munongo or any one of his officers who ordered an attack on the *Albertina*. Or, for that matter, it may have been the pilot of the *Lone Ranger* acting without any orders at all.

The Rhodesian commission had only the pilot's word that his Fouga jet was not in flight on the night of the eighteenth. But they took his word as proof positive that there could have been no air attack at all, since the *Lone Ranger* was the only fighter plane around.

So, if the Rhodesians were placing their bets on "pilot error" as the cause of the crash, they were also stacking the deck of evidence to back them up. Even the observations of those who claimed to have seen a second plane were completely rejected as "unreliable."

The United Nations commission, on the other hand, just wasn't in a wagering mood. It heard all testimony, examined all evidence. It even considered the possibility that the Rhodesians were right—noting, however, that this would imply the poor judgment of all three experienced pilots not once but several times before the expected landing. But, in the end, it was left with an insoluble mystery:

> No evidence of sabotage has come to its attention but the possibility cannot be excluded. . . .
> . . . it cannot exclude attack as a possible cause of the crash.

The attack theory was basically unprovable because it was predicated on the assumption that the *Albertina* was shot down. No bullets or bullet holes were found to support materially any such theory. And no witness who claimed to have seen or heard the planes ever reported hearing the sound of gunfire.

But what if the attack had been not by gunfire but by the attacking plane itself? The Rhodesian report concluded "that the aircraft was allowed by the pilots to descend too

low so that it struck the trees and was brought to the ground."
Conceivably, however, the interference or "buzzing" of a
second plane could have *forced* the aircraft to descend too
low in the darkness.

This possibility, hardly considered at all by any of the
commissions, would account not only for the testimony of
alleged eyewitnesses but also for Sergeant Julien's reference
to the Secretary General having told his crew to "go back."
And it would preclude any trace of an attack. No bullets.
No rockets. The perfect crime of the airways.

As things stand, there are—and will always be—too many
unanswered questions surrounding the mysterious and tragic
death of Dag Hammarskjold that September night.

Edmondbury Godfrey Kn.t mur.d A.D. 16

Portrait of Sir Edmund Berry Godfrey.—*Photograph courtesy National Portrait Gallery, London*

WHO
KILLED
SIR
EDMUND?

---

the
"perfect"
murder
of
Judge Godfrey...

THEY FOUND THE body on Thursday, October 17.

It lay prone in a rainy ditch on Primrose Hill. It was stretched out across the thick brambles, scarcely touching the ground. The head was shaven clean, resting on the elbow of the right arm and facing left. Just beyond, a hat and wig had fallen to the bottom of the ditch.

A sword had been run through the chest and out the back, the tip protruding several inches past a collarbone.

"Lord bless us!" cried one of those who had stumbled onto the scene. "There's a man murdered!"

"Pray God," said another, "it be not Sir Edmund Berry Godfrey."

Hours later, in the flickering light of nearby White House Inn, they knew it was Godfrey. A constable summoned after dark positively identified the judge's body.

What none of them could know, however, was the importance of their discovery. The murder was more than a puzzle to contemporary criminologists; it was a nearly perfect mystery, one that would remain unsolved and probably insoluble over the centuries. More than that, it was a bombshell that would rock the political base of all England and very nearly topple the monarchy of Charles II.

For Godfrey, at fifty-seven, was well known to Londoners both as a judge and as a man of conscience and integrity. In 1665, for example, when the city was in the deadly grip of the plague and men of means fled to the countryside, Godfrey was one of the few public servants who stood fast. "He was," a friend recalled, "the man that stayed to do good and did the good he stayed for." And when a notorious grave robber defied arrest that summer by taking refuge in a plague-ridden hospital, it was Godfrey who risked his life to capture the man and bring him to justice. For his courage and his devotion to duty, Edmund Berry Godfrey was shortly thereafter knighted by the king.

Now, thirteen years later, Sir Edmund lay dead on the

floor of an inn, brutally murdered. And a dozen ale-sipping
patrons crowded round. Carefully they examined his person.
Three gold rings were on his fingers and in his pockets the
startling sum of seven guineas, four broad pieces, and four
pounds in silver (much as if, today, the body of a man were
found in the woods with several hundred dollars in his bill-
fold).

If this were murder, one thing was sure: Robbery was
no motive for it!

But was it murder? Might it not be suicide, instead? The
question naturally arose when the constable visited Godfrey's
surviving brothers later that night. But the mere hint of
suicide outraged the family. In such a case, they knew, the
victim's estate would be forfeited wholly to the crown. Besides, so much of the evidence seemed to refute the charge.
There was no blood on the front of the coat where the sword
had twice punctured Godfrey's chest. True, there was a drop
on the back, near the point of the blade; but that was more
likely the result of having removed the sword from the body
before moving the body to the inn. There was no blood inside the coat, either; but there were bruises all across the
chest, a massive discoloration. There was a hard swelling
under one ear and the purple stripe of a tight band or rope
around the neck. And the neck was broken.

No, the brothers vowed, it had to be murder. No man
could beat himself to a pulp, strangle himself, break his neck
—and *then* commit suicide by impaling himself on a sword.

An autopsy also revealed that Godfrey, voluntarily or in-
voluntarily, had not eaten for two full days before he died.

The brothers' murder theory took hold quickly. Details
were left to public speculation. According to one leading
version, the judge was killed somewhere in London, transported afterward to Primrose Hill, and there propped up to
look as if he'd taken his own life. It was all part of a
dastardly Roman Catholic plot to assassinate the king and
subject his people to the rule of the pope.

On Monday, October 21, 1678, King Charles himself addressed the Parliament. "I now intend to acquaint you," he said, "as I shall always do with any thing that concerns me, that I have been informed of a design against my person by the Jesuits. . . . I will leave the matter to the law and, in the meantime, will take as much care as I can to prevent all manner of practices by that sort of men, and of others too, who have been tampering in a high degree with foreigners, and contriving how to introduce popery amongst us."

That was the magic word! A horror of "popery" had incited Englishmen, particularly Londoners, for more than a hundred years. Laws against the church had been so refined that it was theoretically impossible to practice the Catholic religion.

No Catholic could hold government office or act as executor, administrator, or guardian. None could practice law or medicine. The only Catholics even allowed near London were tradesmen; all others were banished to ten miles beyond the city limits and forbidden to travel more than five miles from home for any reason at all. To convert anyone to the church was high treason. Multiple fines and forfeitures were levied to reduce to pennilessness any Catholic who refused to take the oath of supremacy of the Established Church or who was caught taking part in Catholic ritual or meetings.

"Provided that this does not extend to the Duke of York."

And there was the rub. This exception, appended to the latest piece of legislation that very year, was official recognition that Catholic influence ran deep within the monarchy itself. James Stuart, Duke of York, was Charles' brother and a converted Catholic. He was also heir apparent to the throne so long as Queen Catherine, a Portuguese-born Catholic, remained childless.

All the laws of England might rail against Catholicism, but the next king of England himself was going to be a Catholic. Unless, of course, the line of succession could somehow be changed.

That's where the Earl of Shaftesbury came in. As leader of the opposition Green Ribbon Club, he was committed to bring about such a change. His candidate was the Duke of Monmouth. If Charles would swear to the legitimacy of this illegitimate son, Shaftesbury would be assured of a puppet king in the near future—and a good old-fashioned Protestant puppet at that. In return, he would cooperate with Charles in securing appropriations from Parliament to aid the monarch's ailing treasury.

But Charles said no. So Shaftesbury turned to the people for support and counted heavily on their native fear of popery to win it. It was a minor ploy, one the king felt sure he could overcome.

Then came news of the plot.

It was whispered to the king in St. James Park by Christopher Kirkby, an occasionally employed chemist of the royal laboratories. It was repeated that evening, August 13, louder and with the strident accompaniment of a fanatic clergyman, Israel Tonge. It swelled to peak volume with the testimony of a special witness produced by Tonge several weeks later.

This was September 28. The king's privy council (or cabinet) had been called to consider the merits of Tonge's report on the so-called popish plot. The councillors were especially interested in the charges brought by his special witness, an ex-Jesuit named Titus Oates.

Well, not exactly an ex-Jesuit, he told them, but an Anabaptist minister, anyway, one who had posed as a convert to Catholicism so he could spy on the men of the Jesuit order. What he did not tell them, of course, was of his previous history—of his expulsion from several parishes and from his post as chaplain in the royal navy for what one historian has tenderly called "unnatural practices, not to be named," or of the perjury case still pending against him in his home town of Hastings, where he had leveled malicious accusations against a local schoolmaster.

Nor did the council really care about his private life. The tales he bore were of far greater interest to them. Not only did the Catholics plan the bloody conquest of England and her dominions, he affirmed, but plans were already afoot to assassinate the king. In fact, two men had been hired to shoot him that past March. But they failed to take advantage of the one good opportunity they had and were severely reprimanded and flogged for their neglect.

The following month, he said, a special conference of Jesuits from all over England had met at a tavern in the Strand to discuss alternative means of murder. They decided on poisoning. And Oates had it on good authority that £15,000, a fabulous sum in those days, had been given as a retainer for the job to none other than Sir George Wakeman, the queen's own physician.

This information fitted neatly into the political scheme of things—what with Shaftesbury's eagerness to put the king on the defensive and rally the public behind his own brand of antipopish patriotism. But Oates could not be sure of it at the time. As a matter of fact, he doubted that the privy council would ever take his report seriously enough for an investigation. So he took the precaution of listing his charges in a sworn affidavit, which he presented to a Westminster magistrate one day before the council meeting.

And the magistrate he chose was Sir Edmund Berry Godfrey.

Just, forthright, and honest nearly to a fault, Godfrey would fearlessly pursue the proper line of inquiry. Or so Oates and Tonge thought, anyway. But what they ignored —or did not realize—was the judge's equal reputation for tolerance. There was no priest hunting in his bailiwick, none of the early morning raids on holy mass that were so common in other parts of the city. He had, in fact, made many friends among men of the Catholic faith. One of these was Edward Coleman, secretary to the Duke of York and a figure who loomed large among Oates' charges of treason.

Thus, ironically, the council was fully prepared to act on those charges, while Godfrey, who had been relied on for added support, had reason to falter. As soon as Oates was gone, Godfrey sent an urgent message to Coleman warning him of the peril.

During the days that followed, friends noted the judge's strange behavior. He seemed glum, melancholy, as though deeply worried. None knew of his involvement with Coleman. It was common knowledge, though, that he had taken Oates' deposition; and it was easily presumed that he was in great danger from popish killers.

Godfrey himself blurted out to the Salisbury bishop, Gilbert Burnet, that he feared being struck on the head some night as he walked along the streets of London. He never confided the source of that fear. But he spoke guardedly of a secret, "a dangerous secret," which would be fatal to him. His only security, he said, was the deposition.

"Oates is sworn and is perjured," he insisted to a friend as they walked together near the palace. True enough, the Jesuits had held a conference in the spring, he said, but this was only to discuss the subject of religious tolerance and meant nothing to the king's well-being.

"But there is a design upon the Duke of York," he added, "and this will come to a dispute among them. You may live to see an end on't, but I shall not."

Two days later, on Saturday, October 12, he walked out of his house on Hartshorn Lane and was never seen alive again.

His brothers tried at first to keep the disappearance secret. But word spread quickly. For this was not the London of today, sprawling and dense. It was a city, say, more the size of Memphis, Tennessee. The news that a high-placed, popular judge was missing could not very well be hidden.

By the middle of the following week, rumor was rife. Everyone had his own explanations. Godfrey had secretly, scandalously married a lady of fortune. He had gone off on a debauch with a local prostitute. He had dropped out of sight to escape creditors, perhaps even gone abroad. He had committed suicide. He had been murdered, probably by popish avengers, and was last seen at the Duke of York's palace, at the residence of the king's treasurer, at the palace of the king himself.

Then, they found the body on Primrose Hill.

Overnight the mood of the people turned from fancy to fury. Ballads mourned Godfrey as a martyr. Medals depicted his murder under supervision of the pope. One enterprising craftsman turned out a special dagger with inscriptions on both sides of the blade: "Remember the Murder of Edmond Bury Godfrey" (the name was variously misspelled) and "Remember Religion." He sold 3,000 of them in a single day.

Women slept with small knives under their pillows. Some carried them along whenever they went out. But Lady Shaftesbury herself outdid them all. She had a pair of pocket pistols custom-made to fit her muff, and she kept these with her at all times.

The sequel to this melodrama came swift and violent. The murder was seized upon at once as proof of the popish plot that menaced England. Raids on suspected Catholic sanctuaries were stepped up. Those who doubted the existence of the plot were immediately numbered among the plotters.

Lord Shaftesbury went about zealously taking down evidence for the prosecution—including the testimony of a six-year-old child passed on to him by two teen-age boys. Not that the Green Ribbon chief necessarily believed a word of it, or even the substance of the whole conspiracy charge. What he did, says his biographer, H. D. Traill, "was to take the story as Oates told it, and without believing it . . . to turn .it to his political purposes."

Meanwhile, new and more startling revelations were announced.

"I do accuse the queen," bellowed Titus Oates triumphantly

before the privy council, "for conspiring the death of the king."

Still, when the councillors took him to Catherine's residence at Somerset House, he could not point out the room where he had supposedly overheard her join in that conspiracy. Nor could he reasonably account for having withheld the charge when he first appeared before the privy council.

The king, for his part, would take none of it seriously. He vowed to stand by his queen and angrily denounced those who proposed to have her banished. He listened incredulously to the "true narratives" divulged by William Bedloe and Miles Prance.

Bedloe, a former stable boy and gentleman's gentleman with a bent for larceny, had come forward to claim the £500 reward for identifying Godfrey's killers. He, too, had been to Somerset House, he told a special investigating committee. He had seen the body of the beloved magistrate there in the company of two men. One was an unknown servant of Lord Bellasis—who just happened to be one of London's more prominent Catholics. The other was Samuel Atkins, a young clerk in the office of Samuel Pepys, the noted diarist— who just happened to be a close friend of the Catholic Duke of York.

Atkins was immediately jailed and questioned. Unfortunately for Bedloe, though, he had a perfect alibi for the night in question. Well, answered the informer Bedloe, it was dark in those corridors and easy enough to mistake the man's identity. It must have been someone else.

As it happened, then, a Roman Catholic silversmith named Miles Prance was arrested on information provided by a disgruntled lodger of his in Covent Garden. Half-drunk at a tavern one evening, Prance had protested that three priests about to be hanged were innocent of any popish plot.

Bedloe seized the opportunity. Prance was known to have done occasional work for the queen. It must have been

Prance that night at Somerset House. He swore it was Prance.

Naturally, the silversmith denied the charge. But the committee had already decided against him. They sent him off to Newgate Prison to reconsider his answer. Two nights later, bound in irons on the ice-cold floor of a filthy jail, he gladly reconsidered. That was December 22.

A note from Shaftesbury jogged his memory. The note, slipped under the door of his cell in the dark of night, hinted of a pardon for his cooperation in the matter. Prance was taken to the opposition leader's home that same night, and there discussed the nature of his "cooperation." On the twenty-fourth, he was ready for the privy council.

He had lied earlier, he told them. He knew all about the plot, had even been in on the murder of Godfrey, and was prepared to tell all. He named three men as the actual killers —Robert Green, Henry Berry, and Lawrence Hill. The latter two men were servants at Somerset House. Together, on some pretext, they had lured the magistrate inside. And they had killed him there. Then they took him out to Primrose Hill and staged a suicide.

It was all the public needed to hear. The trials that followed were mere formalities, the hurried ritual of legal practice. The accused were not even offered the right to a fair defense. They were kept in solitary confinement before their trials, deprived of legal counsel and the visits of friends and relatives throughout. They were badgered and insulted by the court when they sought to question witnesses on their own behalf.

First Coleman; then the priests; then Green, Berry, and Hill; then five Catholic members of the House of Lords (including Bellasis); in turn, the innocent were sacrificed at the altar of the people's rage.

In the end, of course, King Charles rode out the storm unharmed. Oates' conflicting testimony eventually belied his story of the plot; Shaftesbury was disgraced by his support of an obvious fraud. And, within a year or so, England began to recover her sanity. But it took the lives of at least a dozen men before the fury of the plot was spent.

Meanwhile, much of the evidence that might have solved the celebrated mystery of Godfrey's death was already lost. All that remained was speculation.

From the first there were those, however few in number, who thought Godfrey a suicide. Roger L'Estrange, the king's historian and pamphleteer, sought desperately during the 1680s to prove the point. He stressed the magistrate's recurring fits of depression, which he seems to have inherited from his father (who *did* commit suicide). He stressed also the worries with which Godfrey found himself burdened: his failure to act upon Oates' accusations when he first heard them, his intimacy with the accused Coleman, his knowledge of "a dangerous secret."

Whatever indications there were of suicide, however, may be readily dismissed. True, the magistrate could have fallen on his own sword. But there were two stab wounds in the body; and it is unlikely he would have fallen on the sword once and, having bungled the job, picked himself up and done it all over again.

Then, too, it is true that he could have hanged himself on a tree limb, probably with his necktie, and succeeded somehow in breaking his neck as he dangled. But how did he get down afterward into the ditch where he was found, his head resting neatly along the crook of his arm?

Either method of suicide might, strictly speaking, have been possible. But the two together make the proposition absurd. No man commits suicide twice!

Possibly, it has been said, the man did commit suicide—one way or the other. His body could have been later rearranged on the hill by someone with a vested interest in having the incident labeled a murder—that is, in such a way as to make the suicide look staged. But this would not account for marks of a severe beating found on his chest;

and it would not account for evidence of his having starved himself or been starved for two full days before he died.

Almost certainly Godfrey was murdered. But by whom? The difficulty is not to find someone with sufficient motive. The difficulty is that, even now, 300 years later, there are so very many suspects from whom to choose.

None of these was Green, Berry, or Hill. The inadequate bits of evidence used against them at the trial coupled with alibis subsequently disclosed on their behalf, assure us of their innocence. Even Prance later recanted his testimony.

To be sure, this does not alone disprove the notion of Godfrey's murder by "popish" elements. By 1678, Catholics were besieged on all sides—by a government whose laws had virtually disenfranchised them, by a rabble-rousing crusade led by Oates and Tonge, by an accumulation of popular prejudices that had developed since the reign of Henry VIII. That they would act quickly and violently to meet any threat to their existence is not entirely out of the question.

What, after all, was that special secret entrusted to Godfrey? Quite possibly it was the same one held by the three priests whom Prance had defended. They were convicted on Oates' word alone. And, though they might have been saved by proving Oates a liar, they went to their deaths rather than reveal their secret: that the big Jesuit conference of which everyone spoke so knowingly was not held at any tavern at all but at the palace of the Duke of York!

If this information were made public, there would be no further dispute of James' succession to the crown. He would be successfully impeached and a lucky man even to escape with his life. This is not to say that he was directly responsible for the murder; but, while historians tend to neglect the possibility, he certainly had a strong interest in silencing Sir Edmund.

On the other hand, any one of those decrying that same popish plot might have been the murderer.

Take Oates. As of the first of October, all he had to rant

about was a plot—an obscure plan to despoil king and country. His evidence was disproved at every turn, his testimony discredited by its own contradictions. (Charles himself thought little of this alleged attempt on his life. When details of it were first presented before the privy council, he excused himself from the meeting and went off to the races at Newmarket, instead.)

What Oates needed was something tangible, something dramatic, anything that would rouse his countrymen to action. What he needed was the murder of a man like Godfrey—a murder staged clumsily and obviously as a suicide—to spark the public indignation and give substance to his charges of a plot.

Remember, too, Godfrey's own claim that Oates had "forsworn himself." Suppose the latter, in the course of his deposition, said something to the magistrate (recorded or not) that later conflicted seriously with what he told the privy council, something that would have caused his public disgrace and downfall. It is possible that this was the "dangerous secret" to which Godfrey later alluded. And it is possible that Oates may thus have had a dual motive for the killing.

But Oates' career was only one beneficiary of the "plot" scare. Another was the political career of Lord Shaftesbury and his green-ribboned coterie in Parliament. Shaftesbury seemed to have everything to gain from Oates' plot and nothing to lose. At best, the panic would unseat James from his place as heir apparent to the king. At worst, the king would be further weakened in his battle with the lords for political supremacy by the need to defend himself on yet another front.

But Shaftesbury had an Achilles heel: His chief lieutenants, he discovered, were actually in the pay of the French king. Yes, those who screamed loudest against the twin menaces of France and Catholicism had been hired to do so by French Catholics as a diversionary action against Charles.

If this were ever disclosed, the opposition would be broken and Shaftesbury personally ruined.

Coleman knew this. As it happened, he was an intermediary between the French ambassador and some of the smaller fry of the Green Ribbon Club. He himself might be loyal enough to the Catholic cause not to divulge the information. But what about Godfrey? Could Coleman have confided it to him after the judge warned him of Oates' deposition? And would Godfrey, a man of high principle and integrity, not take the news straight to the king? Indeed, Shaftesbury had good reason to worry, possibly even a motive for murder.

But why so brutal a murder? Why the beating and the starvation before the *coup de grace*? Are they consistent with the rational approach to murder one might expect of a politician in such a quandary?

Of Oates' aberrant little group one could expect anything, sadism and terror included. But in the case of Shaftesbury, there can be only one answer. Godfrey would most likely have been held for interrogation before his death. How much did he already know? Whom had he told? Interrogation in those days went hand in hand with physical duress.

The evidence is impressive. Still, it would be unrealistic to presume that Godfrey's links to the plot *had* to be the cause of his death. Probably he was murdered, yes, but not necessarily for political reasons. Perhaps the killing was done for personal reasons never examined at the time.

One must include among the list of suspects, then, many others of Godfrey's friends and acquaintances. Perhaps his brothers, for that matter, who stood to gain financially by his death. Or even a grudge-bearing felon whom Godfrey had sent to prison.

From just such a premise the English detective-story writer John Dickson Carr has built an excellent case of circumstantial evidence against the Earl of Pembroke. Pembroke, an alcoholic and sadistic young man about town, had been indicted for murder earlier that year. And the magistrate who prosecuted the case was none other than Godfrey himself. Moreover, the victim in that case had been stamped to death, his chest a mass of bruises much like those later found on Godfrey's body.

Convicted of manslaughter, but not murder, Pembroke was released on a statutory exemption for noblemen. He was, therefore, a free man at the time of Godfrey's death.

But so were many others. Just how many we may never know. For with all the evidence that was forever denied to history through self-serving, blind, fanatic patriotism, the murder of Sir Edmund Berry Godfrey has become a practically insoluble, perfect crime.

Amy Robsart by W. F. Yeames.—*Photograph courtesy The Tate Gallery, London*

QUEEN'S RIVAL, LOVER'S WIFE

---

the
scandalous
death
of
Amy Robsart...

Thus sore and sad that lady griev'd,
   In Cumner Hall so lone and drear,
And many a heartfelt sigh she heav'd,
   And let fall many a bitter tear.

And ere the dawn of day appear'd,
   In Cumner Hall so lone and drear,
Full many a piercing scream was heard,
   And many a cry of mortal fear.

The death-bell thrice was heard to ring,
   An aërial voice was heard to call;
And thrice the raven flapp'd its wing
   Around the tow'rs of Cumner Hall.

The mastiff howl'd at village dorr,
   The oaks were shattered on the green;
Woe was the hour—for never more
   That hapless Countess e'er was seen.

And in that manor now no more
   Is cheerful feast and sprightly ball;
Forever since that dreary hour
   Have spirits haunted Cumner Hall.

(William Mickle)

OF ALL MAN'S motives for murder, surely one of the commonest takes its shape from the triangle of love. Crimes of passion are universal. They are eternal. They add the luster of romance to the plain brutality of an unsolved killing.

And when the hypotenuse of that triangle is none other than the queen of England, the case takes on a historical dimension as well.

So it was, on September 8, 1560, when Amy Robsart was found dead at the foot of the stairs in her country home at Cumnor Place, about three miles from the town of Oxford. She was twenty-eight years old.

Amy was the daughter of Sir John Robsart, a wealthy and highly respected knight of the noble family of Norfolk. She had two brothers, one of them a half-brother by her mother's former marriage. The other was widely known to be illegitimate, though he bore the Robsart name.

Amy, therefore, was considered the natural heiress to her father's estate. Conversely, her death might have been of substantial benefit to the others of the family. Under ordinary circumstances, this benefit would have provided a classic motive for murder.

Circumstances, however, were most *extra*ordinary. For Amy's death served too well the private interests of her husband, Robert Dudley, later Earl of Leicester. All the court seemed alive to rumors of Queen Elizabeth's infatuation with the handsome young man. In fact, one of the more popular versions of the story held that the two of them would long ago have wed had it not been for the simple fact that Dudley was already married—to the fair-complexioned, auburn-haired, and very pretty daughter of Sir John Robsart.

"Lord Robert has come so much into favour," wrote the Spanish ambassador, Count de Feria, in an official report to King Philip II, "that he does whatever he likes with affairs, and it is even said that her Majesty visits him in his chamber day and night. People talk of this so freely that they go so far as to say that his wife has a malady in one of her breasts and the Queen is only waiting for her to die to marry Lord Robert."

The timing of Amy's death, then, was more than opportune. It seemed incredible.

For the last several years, Dudley had spent precious little time at home. He was nearly always with the queen—in her service, at her service.

Their friendship dated back to childhood. But the strength of that bond became evident only upon Elizabeth's ascension to the throne in 1558, at the age of twenty-five. Among her first decrees were those conferring upon young Dudley the highest of honors. He was made a Knight of the Garter, Privy Councillor, and Master of the Horse.

It was a far cry from the brand of treason that had stained his name for generations. His grandfather, Edmund Dudley, had been executed in 1510 on just that charge (although it was mainly to quell public rage against him as the oppressive tax collector for Henry VII). His father, John Dudley, was executed for his part in an abortive attempt to place a sister-in-law, Lady Jane Grey, on the throne. And he himself was committed to the Tower of London in 1553, in the wake of his father's disgrace.

All in all, it had not been a good century for the Dudleys.

By the time of his own imprisonment, Robert Dudley was a married man of twenty-one. His wife, Amy, visited him regularly, providing him with such domestic comforts as the warder's disregard might allow. Once he was released, however, she scarcely saw him at all.

First he was off to France to serve with the English army there. After a year, he returned. But the homecoming was a brief affair. The queen's coronation, which shortly followed, heralded a new dawn in the daily growing fortunes of young Lord Dudley.

Lady Dudley, on the other hand, spent almost no time at court. Nor for that matter did the wives of any of the men serving the queen. For Elizabeth was, by her own admission, quite jealous of her male entourage. She basked in the flattery of their constant, undiverted attention.

She was especially eager for the affections of her favorite, Dudley. And the court was rife with gossip of their love. Bitterness and jealousy filled the air.

Portrait of Robert Dudley, Earl of Leicester.—*Photograph courtesy National Portrait Gallery, London*

All London, it seemed, both despised and envied the man's station. His fortunes soared. Wealth, power, the confidence of the crown—all these were his overnight.

Alvarez de Quadra, the bishop of Aquila who succeeded de Feria as Spanish ambassador, advised Philip very early in 1560 that it would be wise to develop a good and friendly relationship with Dudley. "In Lord Robert," he wrote, "it is easy to recognize the king that is to be."

Later, toward the end of March, he noted: "I have understood Lord Robert told somebody, who has not kept silence, that if he live another year he will be in a very different position from now. He is laying in a good stock of arms, and is assuming every day a more masterful part in affairs. They say that he thinks of divorcing his wife."

Such thoughts, however, if ever they crossed Dudley's mind, soon became unnecessary. For, less than six months later, his wife was dead.

The details of her death were put to a local coroner's jury quite simply: She had slipped, authorities deduced, at the top of the stairs at Cumnor Place; she had fallen and broken her neck. While the jury's verdict was never formally disclosed, it seems safe to surmise that the jurors accepted the inference of death by accidental cause.

No indictments were ever issued in the case. But a great many questions remained unanswered. Why had Dudley sent his wife to their country home in the first place? It was a large and lonely old house that he had only recently rented and almost never visited. And why had Amy dismissed all the servants for that fatal day, September 8? She usually kept one or more at home with her, even on Sunday.

Had Amy dismissed the servants herself? Or had they been sent off by Lord Dudley, instead? What (or who) had caused her fall down the staircase? And would such a fall have been sufficient to result in a broken neck?

How was it that her hood was found in place, undisturbed,

still upon her head despite the mishap?

This last question touches on a point never fully resolved. Twenty years after Amy's death, it was sarcastically noted, in passing, that "she had the chance to fall from a pair of stairs, and so to break her neck, but yet without hurting of her hood, that stood upon her head."

One other matter of some concern was a report attributed to de Quadra that Elizabeth had confided news of Amy's death to him as early as September 3. That date was nearly a week before the actual event.

Some historians have discredited the account on grounds that the ambassador was deliberately trying to stir up feelings against the queen. It is implausible, they say, that Elizabeth, if guilty of such foreknowledge as de Quadra implied, would have been less than clever enough to conceal that guilt. Yet, the rumors of her complicity persisted.

Popular feeling, both at home and abroad, was running strong against her. The English ambassador to Paris, Sir Nicholas Throckmorton, evidenced this distress in a letter to a friend. People everywhere, he said, were beginning "to speak, of the Queen *and some others,* that which every hair on my head standeth at, and my ears glow to hear."

De Quadra was less restrained in reporting the mood of English subjects. "They say," wrote the bishop, "that she and her lover are likely to go to sleep in the Palace and wake in the Tower."

Suspicion fell naturally on Dudley. There was no pretense of grief about him. He did not attend the funeral; he did not appear before the coroner's jury. With an objectivity that seemed to some almost inhuman, he revealed his greatest concern to Thomas Blount, a cousin he had dispatched to clear up the affair at Cumnor.

"The greatness and the suddenness of the misfortune," he wrote, "doth so perplex me until I do hear from you how the matter standeth, or how this evil should light upon me, considering what the malicious world will bruit, as I can take no rest. And, because I have no way to purge myself of the malicious talk that I know the wicked world will use, but one which is the very plain truth to be known, I do pray you, as you have loved me, and do tender me and my quietness, and as now my special trust is in you, that you will use all the devices and means you can possible for the learning of the truth, wherein have no respect to any living person."

It is this candor, this spontaneous expression of self-interest that has persuaded a number of historians of Dudley's innocence in the affair. It's not the way a guilty man would act, they say. He would write of nothing but his sadness and personal loss. He would certainly be present at both the funeral and the courtroom proceedings in order to act out his grief.

Dudley was many things to many people—brash, aggressive, conceited, foolhardy. His character would not have prevented such hypocrisy as might be required to pen the letters of bereavement. Yet, he did not write them. And he did not appear in public.

Elizabeth's own response to intimations of foul play was brief and to the point. "The matter," she notified Throckmorton, "has been tried in the country, and found to the contrary of that [which] was reported."

That which was reported, undoubtedly, was just as Dudley had suspected. He was secretly accused of the death of his wife.

If the jury had, in fact, "found to the contrary," that finding was itself no more than hearsay. No official statement was ever published concerning the verdict. No transcript was even made of the hearings. Such secrecy could only have contributed to the aura of mystery already surrounding the case.

Lending credence to the public's contrary suspicions was a report attributed to Amy's half-brother, John Appleyard. He was said to have informed friends that the jury had returned an open verdict on the case. That is, the jury refused either to convict or to acquit the accused husband. If true, the doubters' doubts were well confirmed.

A short time after the disclosure, one of those same friends told Dudley that Appleyard had been offered large sums of money to reopen the Cumnor incident, "to search the manner of his sister's death." The hint was plain enough: Amy's kinsman presumably knew more than he had told at the inquiry, and for the right price he might now be moved to further testimony. Of course, for the same price, he might also remain unmoved. He did, after all, feel a strong sense of family loyalty.

Dudley had no illusions about public sentiment. It stood hard against him, and he knew it. Appleyard's testimony—true or false—could only hurt him further. Still, he called the man's bluff and won.

The two met at Dudley's home in Greenwich. Their conversation was private. But Thomas Blount, Dudley's cousin, later revealed that when they emerged the widower was visibly angry. He sent Appleyard on his way "with great words of defiance."

Whether the young lord was truly secure in the knowledge of his own innocence or simply playing a bad poker hand well, history will never know for sure. In any case, it worked. Nothing more was heard of Appleyard's consideration of further testimony. And the case was closed.

There were virtually no other suspects from among whom to choose. There had been no robbery. There was no "other man" in Amy's life. There was not even the question of inheritance, since the elder Robsart was still alive.

Even with the daughter dead, no one could say for sure who the principal beneficiary might be. Appleyard was only a stepson, and Amy's "full" brother was illegitimate.

If we presume Dudley's innocence, we are left with neither killer nor motive. We must consider, then, the possibility that Amy's death really was an accident.

True, there was some talk of suicide, but none of it serious. A maid had heard Amy often "pray to God to deliver her from desperation." But that "desperation" may well have been a euphemistic reference to her suffering from cancer—a "malady of the breasts," as it was spoken of freely at the time.

Those who knew her well, including that same maid, swore that so God-fearing a soul as she would never have resorted to the taking of her own life. Nor, we may presume, would anyone choose so clumsy a manner to carry out such a serious intention.

The possibility of an accident has always seemed equally remote. There was, of course, some chance that she might have slipped and fallen down the stairs. But it was unlikely that such a fall would have proved fatal. And the fact that her hood remained in place upon her head would make that kind of accident seem very nearly impossible. At least, it always had until Ian Aird put forth a tentative explanation some four centuries later.

In a 1956 issue of the *English Historical Review,* Aird took serious note of Amy's much discussed cancerous condition. In half of all fatal cases of breast cancer, he pointed out, there are "secondary deposits" in the bones. These make the bones brittle enough to break under ordinary pressure. Furthermore, one out of every sixteen of these cases occurs in the spine, and even the slight strain of walking may at any time cause collapse.

"If that part of the spine which lies in the neck suffers in this way," he continues, "the affected person gets spontaneously a broken neck. Such a fracture is more likely to occur in stepping downstairs than in walking on the level."

Hence, he concludes, it is precisely because of her condition that Amy might well have fallen with her hood intact. The neck would have broken, snapped, almost at once; both head and hood would have maintained their relative positions during the actual descent.

Whatever its causes, though, Amy's death proved more of an obstacle to Dudley's ambitions than their marriage had ever been. It came hard on the heels of two years of widespread gossip and rumor regarding plans to be rid of her. So, to many people, the unkind fate seemed less than natural. And the thought that the queen herself might have had any part in it was more than her subjects could bear.

Elizabeth the woman was strongly attracted to Dudley. But Elizabeth the queen was more detached. She was a Tudor, a child of the cunning Henry VIII. She was too shrewd to play her royal game according to the instincts of her passion.

Reason dictated the alternative course. Almost at once, she dismissed Dudley as a suitor. She continued to favor him with court appointments, eventually conferring upon him the title of Earl of Leicester. She continued privately to harbor her great love for him. But she acted quickly to dissociate her name from his as far as her people were concerned. Indeed, in 1564, she even proposed his name as a likely husband for her cousin and rival, Mary, Queen of Scots.

Elizabeth never married. She lived to reign nearly half a century more, and she had many suitors. But she never even seriously considered one of them, although she knew full well that her death would mean the end of the Tudor line.

Perhaps it was as she had once declared: "I am already married to a husband, which is the people of England." Perhaps, more simply, she could never quite get over her love for—and her loss of—the man Robert Dudley.

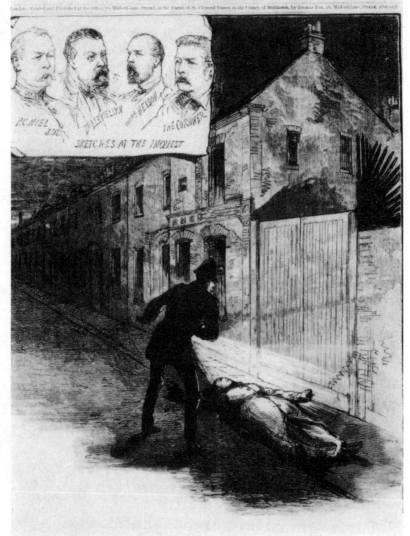

The discovery of Mary Ann Nicholls' body, as depicted in a contemporary London periodical

YOURS TRULY, JACK THE RIPPER

---

*the
scourge
of
London's
East End...*

IT TOOK THEM seven hours to put Mary Jane Kelly back together again.

She had been found in bed on the morning of November 9, 1888. She lay on her back, entirely naked, terribly mutilated, long dead. Her throat had been slit from ear to ear and all the way through to the top of the spinal column. Her face was slashed almost beyond recognition. The ears and nose had been sliced off. The breasts, too, were cut away and placed on a bedside table. The heart and both kidneys had been removed and mounted alongside the breasts. The liver was laid atop the right thigh. The thighs were badly cut. And the lower portion of the body had been excised—including the uterus, which was nowhere to be found.

Four surgeons and an assistant did the job. They worked at it speedily through the morning and early afternoon of the tenth, after the police had finished a preliminary investigation. When they were done, they had a fairly complete corpse to show the coroner's jury. But it was still a very messy corpse.

It was another victim of Jack the Ripper.

The killing excited all parts of the world. But it alarmed England. Queen Victoria dashed off a reproving note to her prime minister, Lord Salisbury.

"You promised when the first murder took place," she reminded him sharply, "to consult with your colleagues about it."

On the morning of the tenth, Salisbury called a full-scale cabinet meeting to discuss the menace. And the elusive Jack was thus accorded a signal honor. He had become—and would remain—the most celebrated murderer in the annals of mystery.

He also became something of a legend.

In the more than eighty years since, the Ripper's crimes have been distorted beyond belief. The madman himself has become virtually a myth, a fantasy of the past. Novels, short stories, plays, operas—all these have told various tales of his hideous doings.

Even Sherlock Holmes got into the act. Typically, the villain in this one, a Spanish imitation of the master called "Jack El Destripador," turned out to be a woman-hating West End doctor who did away with no fewer than thirty-nine comely lasses.

In fact, the Ripper was no woman hater at all. "I am down on whores," he explained in a mocking missive to the press, "and I shan't quit ripping them till I do get buckled."

It was this one class of women he sought out for what he called his "funny little games"; and there was nothing at all lovely about his victims. They were, with one exception, stout, unattractive, middle-aged, ill-clad street brawlers who got terribly drunk when they had the money and took to hustling when they didn't.

Furthermore, Jack seemed to be "down on" whores only in the squalid East End sectors of London. He never struck among ladies of the trade in the gay, fashionable districts to the west. It was always in Whitechapel, Aldgate, Spitalfields —among the poor, the sick, the neglected.

There were no Eliza Doolittles here, none of the cheery Cockney spirit that made them all fair ladies of storybook fame. The neighborhood was tough and mean, and cries of "Murder!" pierced the air nearly every night of the week. Chairs and tables were bolted to the floors of pubs to keep weaponry at a minimum when fights broke out among the men.

Women, too, had their scraps, stripping to the waist and hitting nearly as hard as the men. Children played in the streets half the night so their mothers could offer male guests the privacy of the single room they shared. And gangs terrorized the neighborhood, assaulting old people in the open and extorting money from local prostitutes for their protection or "insurance."

One of those who may not have paid the premiums was Emma Smith. She was found near death one April night, savagely beaten. She died next day. Then there was Martha Tabram. She was stabbed thirty-nine times in early August. No one was convicted of either death. No one was ever tried.

Murder, even unsolved murder, was common enough in those days in the East End. And police efforts were often perfunctory in dealing with it.

Consequently, the authorities could never be absolutely sure when it was that Jack first struck. Nor could they say just how many people he actually killed. He was linked by some to twenty murders during the year 1888. But most educated guesses set the total somewhere between four to seven. This author picks five. The others, it may be said, just weren't his style.

That style, such as it was, soon became horribly evident. First it was Mary Ann "Polly" Nicholls, a prostitute and former inmate of Lambeth Workhouse. Polly had been evicted from her flophouse on Thursday night, August 30. She lacked the money for a night's lodging, so she took to the streets of Whitechapel to get it. Fourpence was the price of her bed, fourpence too the price of her favors.

Presumably she was still out hustling when she met Jack the Ripper. This was about three o'clock in the morning. By four, she lay outside a gateway along Buck's Row (now Durward Street), flat on her back, her throat cut ear to ear.

"The ghastliness of this cut, however," the *Star* reported, "pales into insignificance alongside the other. No murder was ever more ferociously and more brutally done. The knife, which must have been a large and sharp one, was jabbed into the deceased at the lower part of the abdomen, and then drawn upwards, not once but twice. The first cut veered to the right, slitting up the groin, and passing over the left hip, but the second cut went straight upward, along the centre of the body, and reaching to the breast-bone."

Polly's abandoned husband took one look at the body and cried, "I forgive you what you did to me now I find you like this."

Eight days later, the Ripper struck again. This time it was "Dark Annie" Chapman. Her body was found lying in the backyard of a building on Hanbury Street, Spitalfields, less than three-quarters of a mile from the site of the Buck's Row killing. Annie's head was so very nearly severed from her body that the killer had to tie a handkerchief around her neck to hold the whole thing together. She had been left lying on her back, her face turned to the right and the head slightly raised against a wall. Her legs were drawn up, feet on the ground. The left hand rested on the left breast.

The killer showed more than savagery, though. He also showed what the coroner considered an unusual amount of "anatomical knowledge." Not only did he disembowel the corpse, as he had done with Polly. This time he went in after the uterus, no easy surgical task. Skillfully, without causing any internal injury, he removed the organ and took it with him when he left.

Panic struck. A vigilance committee was formed by local tradesmen. Merchants pooled money to offer a reward for the Ripper's capture. Foot patrols were organized among the Reverend Samuel Barnett's collegiate helpers at Toynbee Hall, a settlement house in St. Jude's parish.

As for the police, they made arrests—dozens of them, frantically, indiscriminately. There were two stock brokers on their way out of town for a day's fishing, a loud American tourist, a reporter out tracking the Ripper on his own, sailors, lawyers, doctors. The suspicions proved false in every case, even ridiculous in some cases, pointing up the confusion that reigned at Scotland Yard.

"Blind-Man's Buff," *Punch* labeled it in a feature cartoon.

And the *Times* complained editorially that "they [the police] are at fault, and must apparently await helplessly the perpetration of some fresh outrage to give them a renewed chance of getting on the right track."

It wasn't enough that the killer had utterly baffled the police. Now he took to taunting them.

"Dear Boss," he wrote in a letter to the Central News Agency on September 25, "I keep on hearing the police have caught me but they wont fix me just yet. I have laughed when they look so clever and talk about being on the right track. That joke about Leather Apron gave me real fits." ("Leather Apron" was a poor bootmaker falsely arrested for the murders.)

The psychopathic sense of humor, the supreme self-confidence, the delight in his own notoriety, these were the marks of the menace at large in London: "I saved some of the proper red stuff in a ginger beer bottle over the last job to write with but it went thick like glue and I cant use it. Red ink is fit enough I hope ha ha. The next job I do I shall clip the ladys ears off and send to the police officers just for jolly wouldnt you."

And he signed it "Yours truly, Jack the Ripper." He gave himself the name.

That the police could have so many ghastly, unsolved murders on their hands in one summer was unthinkable. It troubled the Victorian conscience of the upper classes. But to the lower caste among whom the Ripper stalked, it was positively terrifying.

"No one cares what becomes of us," Catherine Eddows told her roommates at a flophouse on Flower and Dean Street. "Perhaps one of us will be next."

Four days later, she was.

It was the early morning of September 30. Eddows had been out drinking that Saturday evening. In fact, she'd had such a good time of it that, by half-past eight, she was literally stretched out across a sidewalk on High Street in a drunken stupor. Two policemen carried her off to Bishopsgate station, and there she was kept under lock and key for four and a half hours to sober up.

When she was released, she asked what time it was. "Too late for you to get any more drink," the desk sergeant chided.

Kate Eddows went off quietly to earn a few pennies before the night was out. A short time later, she was seen talking with a man in Church Passage, off Duke Street. They stood together for some time, presumably until the patrolman on duty had made his latest round. Then, perhaps, they slipped into Mitre Square, a dark and lonely spot—"entered it," as the *Times* put it, "for an immoral purpose." In a matter of minutes, she was dead, butchered by the very man she had feared.

Not only had the face and throat been slashed, but a part of the right ear had been hurriedly cut. "The abdomen was all exposed," the police surgeon added, "the intestines were drawn out to a large extent and placed over the right shoulder. A piece of the intestines was quite detached from the body and placed between the left arm and the body."

And the left kidney was missing.

What distinguished this murder from the Ripper's others, however, was not the brutality of his attack. His "style" was something all London had come to expect of him. What made this crime singularly shocking was the fact that it was only one of a pair that night. Just an hour before, he had done the same job on Elizabeth "Long Liz" Stride outside a noisy clubhouse on Berner Street.

Almost the same job, anyway. He cut her throat while she lay obligingly before him on the ground—the same virtually bloodless slit from one ear to the other. But that was all. The hoofbeats of an approaching pony cart curtailed his savagery. It was Louis Diemschutz on his way to a night job as steward of the International Workmen's Educational Club.

"Little doubt is felt," the *Times* inferred, "from the position of the corpse that the assassin had intended to mutilate it."

Thus frustrated, he hurried over to the vicinity of Mitre Square, a quarter-hour's walk away. There he lured Kate Eddows to her destruction shortly after one-thirty in the morning.

He could hardly contain himself after his dual success. And in a burst of pride he penned another note to the Central News Agency. It was a postcard, and it bore the bloodstains of a long night's work. He mailed it early Sunday.

"You'll hear about Saucy Jacky's work tomorrow," he boasted. "Double event this time. Number one squealed a bit. Could'nt finish straight off. Had not time to get ears for police."

The police, meanwhile, had their own problems. News of "Saucy Jacky's work" made the headlines of Monday's papers, rocking London like a bomb. Public outrage soared—and with it a bitter sense of helplessness in the face of such atrocity. The incompetence of Scotland Yard was universally deplored.

More than once the local coroner had denounced police investigations as bungling and stupid. To begin with, he noted, the constable who examined the scene of the first murder did his job so haphazardly that he never even knew the victim had been "ripped" at all but took the job for a simple throat slitting. Then, when at last the police got the body inside for a post-mortem, they carefully cleaned it before the doctor could arrive—thus washing valuable evidence right down the drain. Not only that; but, after having been reprimanded for this procedure, they did precisely the same thing when they got their hands on the body of poor Annie Chapman.

Even before the Chapman case, the *Star* had made its own sentiments plain enough. "Sir Charles Warren, says the gossips, is going to take the hint pressed on him from every quarter, and will resign," it reported. "The news is almost too good to be true; but it comes from the headquarters of the police, where Sir Charles has nearly as many enemies as there are officials."

Sir Charles was a military man, an ex-general in the Royal Engineers when he became commissioner in 1886. At once, he set himself the task of reorganizing the metropolitan force along the same strict military lines to which he was accustomed. Officers were brought in from the army to staff top police posts. Lengthy reports were filed on such issues as the need for modernized boots and truncheons. But good old-fashioned detective work, the specialty of the Yard's CID (Criminal Investigation Department), was virtually ignored.

What counted with Warren was power—the same massive, uniformed power that was called out to crush an unemployment protest two years later. "Bloody Sunday," it was called. And the memory of those who were killed and injured in the wake of Warren's needless attack assured the new commissioner the everlasting hatred of the working class.

Warren's insistence on military manner rankled even veteran police officers. Finally, in August, 1888, just on the verge of the Ripper's rampage, Assistant Commissioner James Monro resigned in disgust. As CID head, Monro was one of few men experienced in the fledgling science of crime detection. He was probably the one man in all England who might have brought "Saucy Jacky" to justice.

As Monro's replacement, Sir Charles chose Robert Anderson, a socialite lawyer who accepted the appointment eagerly and then went off for a month's vacation in Switzerland. By the time he got back, on October 1, four women were already dead at the Ripper's hands.

The fifth was Mary Jane Kelly. And she was the exception in more ways than one. She was tall, robust, and as tough a woman as ever set foot in the East End. Better known among her colleagues as "Black Mary," she was distinguished from them by her good looks and her vitality. She was young—only twenty-four at the time of the murder—and she was murdered inside her Dorset (now Duval) Street apartment on the morning of November 9.

Time of the murder was later fixed at somewhere between three and four o'clock. At three-thirty, another woman tenant was awakened by the faint cry, "Oh, murder!" Such was the character of the neighborhood that she ignored the cry and simply dropped off to sleep again.

Black Mary's body was spotted by a rent collector through a broken window at the rear of the building. It was just before noon. He fetched the landlord. The landlord summoned a police inspector, the inspector his superintendent and a police surgeon. Then, they went into the room together.

"On the bed lay the body as my man had told me, while the table was covered with what seemed to me to be lumps of flesh," the landlord later recalled. "It looked more like the work of a devil than of a man."

In many ways, it was the gruesome climax of that devil's work.

Enjoying the safety of an indoor setting, the killer took his time carrying out this boldest, goriest, yet most methodical of all his dissections. Nothing in the room showed any signs of violence. The woman lay nude on the bed, evidently of her own accord. Her clothes were arranged neatly by the bed. The organs and appendages of her damaged body were carefully set in a row on the table.

After that, the Ripper struck no more.

Had he had enough, or was he himself killed according to the whim of chance? Did he kill himself? Had he gone abroad? Was he committed to a mental hospital for other manifestations of his insanity? Or jailed perhaps for some other, lesser crime?

The fact that he was gone was a blessing to the poor women in and around Whitechapel. But it was no credit to police ingenuity. In fact, the investigation of Mary Jane Kelly's death had the makings of a real farce.

It began with a pair of bloodhounds. Commissioner Warren had procured the animals in October, a week after the double slaying. They were to be used in trapping the Ripper on the occasion of his next crime. But trial runs did not make the prospect promising. At the first—with Sir Charles himself as the object of the chase—the dogs consistently failed to get their man. Nine days later, they tried again.

"It is stated," the *Times* reported on October 19, "that Sir Charles Warren's bloodhounds were out for practice at Tooting yesterday morning and were lost. Telegrams have been despatched to all the metropolitan police stations stating that, if seen anywhere, information is to be immediately sent to Scotland Yard."

These embarrassments, however, did not deter the commissioner. He put his men on notice, that, in the event of another murder, nothing was to be touched until the hounds arrived. So, for several hours on November 9, while they might have been putting themselves onto the killer's scent, the police merely cordoned off the courtyard around Black Mary's apartment house and waited. Eventually, they learned the dogs had been returned to their owner even before the murder, and that orders for their use were long since cancelled. And, after that, they learned that Sir Charles himself had resigned from the force.

The carnival atmosphere surrounding this latest episode was heightened by the approach nearby of the Lord Mayor's inaugural procession—a colorful and lively affair in its own right. But the shouts of newsboys broke it up by midafternoon, and public attention was diverted to headlines of the Kelly killing.

"The murderer chose his time well," said the *Star*. "He got his sensation."

There were those, however, who didn't think the murderer chose his time at all. He always struck toward the end of the week. Maybe his timing was dictated by the fact that he was an out-of-towner—or, preferably, a foreigner—and spent only certain weekends in the city. Maybe, for example, he was a butcher on one of the many cattle boats coming up the Thames each week. These boats generally docked on Thursdays or Fridays and departed for the continent on Sundays and Mondays. Not only would the boat schedules account for the regularity of his timing; but the nature of his work would prove consistent with his awful crimes.

There was nothing new about the butcher theory. It was held by many from the first. The Spitalfields sector was the home of London's slaughterhouses. It abounded with skilled butchers—so suspiciously abounded with them that Scotland Yard planted detectives among them to locate the killer. They came up with a small, harmless man named Jacobs, who— even after he was quickly and routinely cleared—was chased by angry mobs labeling him the Ripper. In time, the man was literally driven out of his mind by the harassment and had to be locked up anyway.

Flames of anti-Semitism were eagerly fanned by the new CID chief, Assistant Commissioner Anderson. "I am almost tempted," he later wrote in his memoirs, "to disclose the identity of the murderer. . . ."

He didn't, of course. But he did describe him as a low-class Polish Jew. Most likely, the reference was to a local boot-maker, John Pizer, who was taken into custody for the murder of Dark Annie Chapman.

It was the arrest of this man Pizer, alias "Leather Apron," that Jack the Ripper said "gave me real fits." Pizer, however, had an air-tight alibi and was released within forty-eight hours.

Moreover, Anderson denied the authenticity of the Ripper's letters. Indeed, here too he was tempted to divulge the name of the "enterprising London journalist" who had concocted them; here too he refrained.

If Anderson had his pet theory, so did other officials at Scotland Yard have their own. A favorite among them pinned the murders on a well-respected, Oxford-educated lawyer, the son of a prominent surgeon, who committed suicide by jumping into the Thames at the height of his madness.

The theory shocked Victorian sensibilities. It was almost inconceivable that any Englishman—especially a well-bred Englishman—could be responsible for such heinous crimes. It was easier and far more popular to blame them on the inhumanity of a foreign doctor practicing in the East End of London. The knowledge of anatomy, the skill in wielding a knife—these might certainly indicate the work of a medical man. And London Hospital was right in the midst of the murder scenes, on Whitechapel Road.

The doctor theory has been carried a step further by some, alleging that the Ripper was after the Kelly woman all the while for her role in the death of his syphilitic son. He had to kill the others to keep his inquiries of her whereabouts a secret. And he savaged all their bodies in the madness of his vengeance, for he was truly "down on whores."

Nearly a century later—in November, 1970—the late London surgeon Thomas E. A. Stowell broadly hinted that he knew who the murderer was. His suspect involved none other than Edward, Duke of Clarence, grandson of Queen Victoria, and, if he had lived, heir to the throne of England. That conclusion was based on disclosure of an entry in the diary of Sir William Gull, royal physician at the time of the killings: "Informed blank that his son was dying of syphilis of the brain." Dr. Stowell, in his eighties at the time of this disclosure and a lifelong student of the Ripper mystery, was a childhood friend of the physician's daughter, from whom he allegedly obtained knowledge of the document.

On the other hand, one amateur detective, an artist named William Stewart, has proposed that the killer wasn't a man at all but a woman, instead—a midwife, perhaps, with a pretty good knowledge of surgery herself. Others have considered the possibility of similarly "invisible" killers, people whose presence would not have attracted attention and who might even have had a good excuse if found still hovering over a victim's body. A priest, for example. Or, better yet, a policeman.

Even the budding young playwright and critic George Bernard Shaw got his two cents' worth in. In a letter to the *Star* on September 24, he reminded readers that slum conditions in London's East End had been loudly decried by socialists for years—all to no avail. Yet, one Ripper, in just a matter of weeks, had roused sufficient public and newspaper interest for the possibility at last of real reform.

"Whilst we conventional Social Democrats," he noted with typically outrageous sarcasm, "were wasting our time on education, agitation and organization, some independent genius has taken the matter in hand, and by simply murdering and disembowelling four women, converted the proprietary press to an inept sort of communism."

Nor did press attention wane. Even when he was through, stories about "Saucy Jacky" kept cropping up. He was the notorious poisoner George Chapman, the sexual fetishist Thomas Cutbush. He was an Algerian in New York City accused of killing a waterfront prostitute called "Old Shakespeare."

Best of all, he was a mad Russian doctor sent to London by the czar's secret police to expose the incompetence of Scotland Yard to public ridicule.

But for all these "solutions," the villain's identity remained a riddle. He excited the public imagination but never satisfied it. He deftly eluded every trap the police set, defied every effort to track him down.

Still, he led a merry chase. And all along the way he teased his hunters playfully:

> I'm not a butcher, I'm not a Yid,
> Nor yet a foreign skipper,
> But I'm your own light-hearted friend,
> Yours truly, Jack the Ripper.

Portrait of Louis XIV in 1685 in the museum at Versailles.—Photograph courtesy la Réunion des Musées Nationaux

GRAND DISGUISE

---

the
Man
in
the
Iron Mask . . .

SOME SAID HE was a son of King Charles II, others of Charles' governing predecessor, Oliver Cromwell. By turns, he was the English Duke of Monmouth, the French Duc de Beaufort, even the celebrated playwright Molière!

He was the Man in the Iron Mask, a romantic creation of the novelist-dramatist Alexandre Dumas. And in the last adventures of Dumas' eternally popular d'Artagnan, swashbuckling captain of the musketeers, he was nothing less than a twin brother of Louis XIV. An abortive attempt to replace his brother as king of France cost him his freedom. He was condemned to prison for life, his face masked to hide forever the fraternal likeness.

The story was the product of a century and a half of rumor. It derived not only from peasant lore but also from the writings of some highly regarded men of letters.

In fact, it was another French novelist-dramatist, the renowned Voltaire, who first publicized "details" of the mask in an essay written in 1756:

> . . . On the journey the prisoner wore a mask, the chin-piece of which had steel springs to enable him to eat while still wearing it, and his guards had orders to kill him if he uncovered his face. He remained on the island [Ile Sainte-Marguerite] until an officer of the secret service by name Saint-Mars . . . brought him to the Bastille still wearing his mask. . . . He was a wonderfully well-made man, said his physician; his skin was rather dark; he charmed by the mere tone of his voice, never complaining of his lot nor giving a hint of his identity.

In his later writings, Voltaire was less subtle in suggesting the prisoner's origins. "The Man in the Iron Mask," he finally declared, "was no doubt an elder brother of Louis XIV."

Voltaire's political purposes in telling the tale are not altogether clear; and the facts of his historical assertions are not always faultless. But this exposé intensely gripped the public imagination. Eventually, perhaps inevitably, that same imagination carried the possibilities of such a relationship beyond even the classic fiction of Dumas.

The Mask, some said, was not a brother of Louis XIV at all. He *was* Louis XIV.

At least, he should have been. He was the rightful heir to the throne when his father, Louis XIII, died in 1643. But he had been deprived of ascension in favor of a half-brother, the son of Queen Anne and Cardinal Mazarin, and imprisoned at an early age to safeguard the secret. He had, however, been permitted to take a wife sometime later; and she, in turn, bore him a son who was raised on the Mediterranean island of Corsica under the name of "de Buono Parte." That son marked the emergence of a new branch of the family tree, one that would soon give rise to the great Napoleon Bonaparte!

However well it may have served Napoleon as successor to the Bourbon throne, the legend of the Mask did have some basis in historical fact. As early as October 15, 1711, the Princess Palatine wrote, in a letter to her cousin, "A man lived for long years in the Bastille, masked, and masked he died there. Two musketeers were by his side to shoot him if ever he unmasked. He ate and slept in his mask. There must, doubtless, have been some good reason for this, as otherwise he was very well treated, well lodged, and had everything given to him that he wanted. He took the Communion masked; was very devout, and read perpetually."

The story fascinated the social set of the early eighteenth century and fast became a leading topic of drawing-room conversation. Yet, without the publicity of Voltaire's political concern and Dumas' brilliant melodrama, even the idea of one man's strange incarceration might well have receded into the obscurity of passing time.

Instead, the mystery has well endured. It has been handed

down over the centuries with a growing sense of importance. And, today, no historian of Versailles can quite ignore it.

Who was the Man in the Iron Mask? And why was he in prison? Why was his imprisonment such a closely guarded secret? And, most of all, why was he masked? Too many pieces of the puzzle are still missing; and the puzzle as a whole becomes more taunting the longer it remains unsolved.

All we really know, officially, is that he was brought to the Bastille in 1698, when Saint-Mars was transferred from Sainte-Marguerite to become governor of that historic fortress; that he was held virtually incommunicado and always under heavy guard; and that he died there five years later. His death was recorded in the local register at St. Paul's Church on November 19, 1703, under the name "Marchioly." His age was given as "about 45."

The vital statistics were almost certainly false, so that the true identity of the prisoner might remain unknown in death as in life. But the name gave rise to speculation that the Mask was, in reality, the Italian Count Ercole Antonio Mattioli.

This theory subsequently gained credence from reports that Louis XV had told his mistress, Mme de Pompadour, that the prisoner was the minister of an Italian prince. Louis XVI was said to have related much the same story to Marie Antoinette, more specifically identifying him as a "Mantuan intriguer."

Mattioli had been personal secretary to the Duke of Mantua. In July, 1679, he was arrested by the French for conspiracy. He was actually kidnapped on Italian soil and taken to Pignerol, a fortress-prison on the French side of the border.

Neither his crime nor his arrest was any secret. He had betrayed his employer's private negotiations with Louis XIV to deliver the border town of Casale to the French and thus caused great embarrassment for all parties to the agreement. (Three years later, a pamphlet was published under the title *La Prudenza Trionfante di Casale,* describing in detail the arrangements of that same plan which he had so dangerously disclosed.)

"He has been regarded as the mysterious Man in the Iron Mask," acknowledges the historian Andrew Lang, "but for years after his arrest, he was the least mysterious of State prisoners."

Indeed, there is every reason to believe that Mattioli died at Sainte-Marguerite, the prison to which he was transferred when Pignerol was surrendered to the Italians. This was in 1696—long before the Mask showed up in the Bastille!

During his brief stay at Sainte-Marguerite, Mattioli was one of very few prisoners permitted to have a valet in attendance. Perhaps, in the end, he was the only one. For, after an official notation that a "prisoner with a valet" had died in January, 1696, there is no record of any inmate having a servant of his own.

More likely, as many historians agree, the title of the Mask belonged to the valet himself, if not Mattioli's then some other imprisoned there. All signs point to a man known only as Eustache Dauger.

Dauger, too, had begun his term in Pignerol. He was delivered there in 1669, some ten years earlier than Mattioli. In a letter addressed personnally to Saint-Mars and dated July 19, 1669, the king's war minister, Marquise de Louvois, stressed the unusual importance attached to this new prisoner. All precautions were to be taken to prevent any communication between him and anyone he might encounter. No one must pass by his windows. The guards themselves must be separated from him by several doors. The governor was to wait upon the prisoner, threatening him with death if he should ever speak of anything but his daily needs.

Curiously, Louvois ends the letter, "He is only a valet and does not need much furniture." Such concern for a humble valet!

The minister's orders inspired no end of diligence on Saint-Mars' part. As much as twenty years later, for example, on the occasion of his transfer to Sainte-Marguerite, the governor had a special "carriage" built for Dauger's transportation. This was a sedan chair covered with oilcloth and carried by relay teams of four men. For the traveler it must have been much like riding in a steamer trunk. And the trip lasted twelve days!

While the prisoner was at Sainte-Marguerite, an incident occurred that, according to Voltaire, caused much consternation among officials there and reflected their tremendous concern for security:

> One day the prisoner wrote something with his knife on a silver plate and threw it out of the window in the direction of a boat lying by the bank almost at the foot of the tower. A fisherman, to whom the boat belonged, picked up the plate and carried it to the governor. In amazement the latter asked him, "Have you read what is written on this plate, and has anyone seen it in your hands?" "I cannot read," replied the fisherman, "I have just found it, and no one else has seen it." The peasant was detained until the governor was convinced that he had not read it and that the plate had not been seen. "Go now," he said to him; "you are a very lucky man not to be able to read."

And Lang recounts the private testimony of Bastille guards "that all the Mask's furniture and clothes were destroyed at his death, lest they might yield a clue to his identity."

But who was Eustache Dauger? And what had he done to deserve this attention?

Saint-Mars himself was guilty of spreading many of the rumors that began to capture public fancy after the official death of "Marchioly" in 1703. One of these concerned a supposed son of the English Puritan leader, Oliver Cromwell. Another centered on the Duc de Beaufort, a legitimized grandson of Henry IV and erstwhile political intriguer—all told, as colorful and popular a figure as one can find in all of French history.

As it happened, Beaufort went into battle in Crete on June 25, 1669, and was never seen again dead or alive! Many later thought it highly significant that his disappearance coincided so nicely with the appearance of Dauger at Pignerol. Chances are, though, that he was killed in battle, as officially proclaimed, defending the foreign interests of his king against Turkish aggressors.

Who, then, was this Eustache Dauger? All we have left to us through history is the name and name alone. No face, no past. As much a mystery as ever.

The answer would seem to lie in some dark and dangerous secret of the Empire. It must somehow be entwined, inextricably entwined, in the personal or political life of Louis XIV himself. And what a life it was!

"L'état, c'est moi!" the king once declared in a burst of passion. "I am the state!"

It was no idle boast.

His was *le grand siècle*, the century of French splendor, power, and glory. No monarch in European history ever reigned longer, none more powerfully. He shared his authority with no one—not with any counselor, as his father had employed Richelieu, nor with the noblemen of the court.

True, there had been the powerful Cardinal Mazarin, adviser and prime minister to Louis' mother, Anne of Austria. But when Mazarin died in 1661, Louis took full charge. And he had no intention of relinquishing the reins of power once they were in his grip. He drew the lines of his authority almost at once, announcing his decision as his own prime minister. As if to reinforce that authority, he increased the size of the army by a substantial margin.

More importantly, he tried to unify the forces. He took them out of the fragmented command of the country's noblemen and brought them within a previously unheard-of framework of centralized control—his own control from the palace at Versailles!

His government was filled with career officials of the middle class. Unlike noblemen, the bourgeoisie would have no aspirations to such power as might rival that of the king. They would *serve* the king.

An example of one who would not serve was the Count Nicolas Fouquet. Under Mazarin, Fouquet had performed efficiently as finance minister. In fact, he had performed so efficiently that, by the age of thirty-seven, he had amassed a huge personal fortune. The cardinal's death left open a position he dared hope to fill. He would be the young king's prime minister.

In an effort to ingratiate himself at the start, he held a week-long festival in honor of Louis' coronation. Six thousand guests filled his palatial Vaux-le-Vicomte, an estate unexcelled in its magnificence in all of France. The table service was of gold, the music by the famed court violinist Lully, a play by Molière. The financial substance behind such a production was not lost on the king. He was visibly impressed, but not quite as favorably as his host might have hoped. When the party was over, he ordered Fouquet's arrest on charges of malfeasance and treason; and the ambitious politician was hustled off to Pignerol to begin serving a life sentence.

Later attempts to link Fouquet with the Mask have long since been discredited by evidence that he died in that border fortress in 1680.

Instead, historians have tended to connect the Mask with some aspect of contemporary French foreign policy. More often than not, it comes down to the matter of Louis' clandestine dealings with Charles II of England. Certainly this was one of the most exciting and long-lasting diplomatic duels of modern times.

Louis had tried repeatedly during his war against the Hapsburgs to seize the Spanish Netherlands. But he was thwarted on each occasion by a strong alliance of England, Sweden, and the United Provinces. However, in 1670, eleven years after the Peace of the Pyrenees, he signed the highly secret Treaty of Dover that guaranteed England's nonparticipation in such an alliance in the future.

All it took was money.

For here was Charles faced with strong parliamentary unrest, yet terribly handicapped in his resistance. Parliament, by then, had control of the government's purse strings. And the English legislators kept their king on an austerity budget they hoped would force him to relinquish further power.

Louis, on the other hand, was in a strong financial position. He could, to a large extent, support both the French and English monarchies. Charles, in return, had only to make a complete about-face and ally with him in his wars on the United Provinces, support his claims to Spanish territory, and help to reestablish Catholicism in England.

Charles entrusted his part in negotiations leading up to the Dover *entente* to his sister Henrietta. She was more than just a personal favorite. She was wise, and she was shrewd. Conveniently, she was also a sister-in-law of Louis XIV.

But there were others involved in the bargaining. At least there was one other, to whom Charles always referred in correspondence as "the Italian." In a study published in 1912, Monsignor A. S. Barnes concluded that "the Italian" was one Abbé Pregnani. The abbé had served many times before as Charles' envoy in delicate matters of diplomacy. This time, however, his secret dealings were cut short when he was arrested by French authorities on charges of espionage.

Barnes further identifies Pregnani as a natural son of King Charles—a fact, he says, Louis himself did not know until it was too late. Long after the arrest, therefore, Pregnani was forced to don a full-face mask to prevent recognition.

Like so many others, Barnes' story is highly entertaining. Unfortunately, it has long since proved untenable. Historians have found positive evidence that the Abbé Pregnani was alive and well in Rome in 1674 and that he never left the Italian capital from that date on.

It is possible, though, that he might have had an accomplice —a valet, perhaps—who was captured and imprisoned in his stead. And that accomplice might well have been the mysterious Eustache Dauger.

A stronger candidate for the title of the Mask, however, is Andrew Lang's own choice, an English valet named Martin. His master, Roux de Marsilly, was a French Huguenot who had been privy to the secret negotiations between England and France. More than that, he was hard at work to see that they failed.

Marsilly had joined with the Dutch ambassador in trying to form a Protestant league to oppose the religious interests of the French government. He had access to King Charles through direct dealings with the English secretary of state, Lord Arlington. He had every reason to think he had Charles' full support in the venture.

What was worse, Louis thought so too. At least, the French king suspected his English counterpart of playing both ends against a diplomatic middle in a bid for time and money.

Like Mattioli, Marsilly was kidnapped by Louis' henchmen on foreign soil and brought back to France. A letter cited by Lang and dated "Paris, May 25, '69" details the incident:

> The Cantons of Switzerland are much troubled at the French King's having sent 15 horsemen into Switzerland from whence the Sr de Maillé, the King's resident there, had given information of the Sr Roux de Marsilly's being there negociating the bringing the Cantons into the Triple League by discourses much to the disadvantage of France, giving them very ill impressions of the French King's Government, who was *betrayed by a monk that kept him company* and intercepted by the said horsemen brought into France and is expected at the Bastille.

It is just possible that the monk in question is the same "mad monk" to whom Saint-Mars refers as Mattioli's cell-mate ten years later. Marsilly himself was tortured and publicly executed on a trumped-up charge of rape to avoid public disclosure of state secrets.

As we know, Louvois wrote Saint-Mars on July 19 to expect a valet of the utmost political importance. Lang's guess is that they must be one and the same, Martin and this new arrival at Pignerol.

Quite likely, he's right about it. He could be right, too, in supposing the valet to be the notorious Man in the Iron Mask—if only by the process of elimination.

But the larger question looms over this as over so many of the older theories: Why the mask?

We may be able to discount the likelihood of identifying Mattioli as the unknown prisoner, since the crime of his indiscretion was so well known. But what of Marsilly's secret crime? Or even Martin's knowledge of it? What could Martin's face possibly reveal in the way of a diplomatic plot? Could there be anything about any crime that would justify such an unusual measure as covering the prisoner's face for life?

The mask itself is the essence of the mystery, and none of the traditional theories has ever been able to account for it. However, one British historian-journalist recently took another guess; and, while it may seem terribly far-fetched, it does at least put all the pieces of the puzzle together.

In a BBC broadcast in 1955, Hugh Ross Williamson first mentioned the theory. A friend, Lord Quickwood, was credited with its conception.

By 1637, according to Ross Williamson, King Louis XIII and Queen Anne had been married for twenty-two years. In all that time, they had not produced a natural heir to the Bourbon throne. It was fast becoming something of a state crisis. Court gossip suggested that the king might be impotent. More likely, though, the royal couple just didn't get along well enough for any intimate relationship between them. In fact, during all those twenty-two years, they had lived apart for a total of fourteen years. The remaining eight were not spent altogether fondly.

The chances for a child were thus remote. The only thing the king and queen passionately shared was a dislike for the king's younger brother, the Duc d'Orléans. And Orléans, at that point, was next in line to succeed Louis on the throne.

The possibility of such a succession was anathema to Richelieu as well. To prevent it he tried hard to bring about a reconciliation between the royal couple. But all his efforts were in vain. Anne wanted nothing to do with Louis, and Louis could not have cared less.

As an alternative, the cardinal presented a most unusual solution. Queen Anne would bear the king a child, but the king need not be the child's true father. He, Richelieu, would select a vigorous young man of the realm to sire their "natural" heir.

And, of course, it would all be done for the good of the state!

As it happened, the child of that union, later to be called Louis XIV, bore a remarkable resemblance to his sire. Public notice of the likeness would almost certainly have led to political chaos. The true father, therefore, had to be persuaded to leave the country. Appeals were made to both his patriotism and his pocketbook; and, in the end, he made his departure, quite possibly bound for Canada.

After Anne's death in 1666, he came back. He may have been longing all the while to return to his homeland. Or he may have actually hoped to blackmail the ministers of state for additional payments. In any case, his sudden appearance alerted them all to the danger that he might at any time make public the claim of his paternity. So he was promptly arrested, hustled off to prison under the tightest security arrangements that could be devised, and forbidden to speak with anyone on pain of death. His face was covered with a black velvet mask to prevent recognition.

(An interesting sidelight might be considered in connection with this proposition. The very name Eustache Dauger has all kinds of etymological implications. The French verb *"auger"* means "to hollow out," while *"d'auger"* would introduce the preposition "of." The name would also read like a play on the word *"daguer,"* meaning "to stab." The given name "Eustache" is taken from the French word for a cheap sort of clasp knife that might be used either "to stab" or "to hollow out.")

If true, Ross Williamson's story would make the Mask well over eighty years old at the time of his death in 1703. It's not impossible; but it's not likely, either. Even Quickwood has said that the story is nothing more than "a very good guess."

In the end, we are faced with a possibility no less fantastic than anything such scholars as Voltaire, Barnes, or Lang ever concocted. And yet the facts accommodate the fiction—if fiction it be—far better than the "logic" of history's alternative solutions.

Portrait in pastel of Louis XVII by Kucharski in the museum at Versailles.—*Photograph courtesy la Réunion des Musées Nationaux*

LOST
DAUPHIN

---

*the
unknown
fate
of
Louis XVII ...*

IT WAS A simple epitaph:

> Temple Section. June 10, 1795. Louis Charles Capet, ten years two months old, son of Louis Capet, last King of the French, and of Marie Antoinette Josèphe Jeanne of Austria. The deceased was born at Versailles, and died day before yesterday at three o'clock in the afternoon.

It was simple. It was final. It was the end of an epoch.

The French Revolution had transformed the nation completely. Signs of it were everywhere—in the streets, where monuments to royalty lay in the ruin of contempt; on the lips of the people, who addressed one another as "Citizen"; in the very motto from which it drew its justification—*liberté, fraternité, égalité.*

All that remained of the days of the monarchy was the royal family itself. Since August, 1792, its four members had been safely locked away.

They were jailed in the Temple, a cluster of buildings that stood imposingly on the site of what is today a second-hand clothing market on the Square du Temple in Paris. Built in the middle of the thirteenth century, the Temple served as headquarters of the powerful religious-military Order of the Templars and housed some 4,000 people. (Later, under Napoleon Bonaparte, it would be demolished to prevent its ever becoming a shrine to the monarchy—something of an irony inasmuch as its original occupants lived completely and defiantly independent of the crown.)

Of the four captives of the new Republic, only the Princess Marie Thérèse would survive. The others died by turns.

First her father, King Louis XVI—or "Citizen Capet," as he was then called—was tried for treason by the newly created Convention of the Republic. He was found guilty, and guillotined on January 21, 1793. His wife, Marie Antoinette, who had become something of a legend in her own time, met a similar fate less than nine months later.

Until midsummer, however, the dauphin, Louis Charles, and his sister had remained with their mother in the humblest of quarters. Then, on the night of July 3, while the young boy lay sleeping, a shawl over his eyes to keep out the light, six officers entered with disturbing news.

"We have come," said one of them, "to notify you of the order whereby the son of Capet is to be separated from his mother and family."

What followed was a tragicomic scene of struggle in which a determined Marie Antoinette clung desperately to the body of her son while the officers tried as politely as possible to wrest control.

"You would better kill me than take my child from me!" she challenged. And she held them off for the better part of an hour, while they continued to tug, threaten, and insult.

"At last," the princess later recorded, "they threatened even the lives of both him and me, and my mother's maternal tenderness at length forced her to this sacrifice."

The eight-year-old Louis Charles was given first to the care of a cobbler named Antoine Simon. And while it cannot be said definitely that this guardian actually mistreated him, the care afforded him was certainly negligible. Orders were strict, punishment swift. A few contemporary reporters went so far as to reveal a streak of utter sadism in the guardian—or "tutor," as he was euphemistically designated.

The arrangement lasted six months. In January, 1794, Simon resigned custody of the boy. Or, rather, it was decided that, in order to remain faithful to the ideals of the new democracy, Temple officials should not permit Louis Charles the "privilege" of a tutor. After all, no other prisoner had tutors or servants of any kind.

So the cobbler was replaced by a committee of four guards, to be changed daily. And the dauphin was consigned to isolation in a small, dark room at the top of the Temple.

The only furniture in his room consisted of a bed, a table,

and a chair or two. There were no windows, only an iron grating over the door. The door itself was reinforced with steel plates and padlocks. Food and linens were passed to the child through the grating. And even the linens were denied him when, in time, he became too lazy to return those which were soiled.

Days were dim. The nights were dark and lonely. The room went uncleaned, and the filth mounted. The guards themselves kept their distance so as to avoid the stench. The room came alive with all kinds of vermin.

Louis Charles' health had never been good. He was a small, delicate child, frequently ill. At the hands of his captors, he grew steadily worse.

On December 19, 1794, Jean Baptiste Harmand paid a surprise visit to the Temple. Harmand, a revolutionist who shared in management of the Paris police department, was shocked by the condition of the prisoner, who during the period of his detention had developed tumors—one on the elbow of his right arm, another at the wrist.

"The young prince," he reported afterward, "when standing upright, looked not only as if he was deformed, but as if he was suffering from rickets; his legs, thighs and arms were very long and thin; his bust was short; he was chicken-breasted, and his shoulders were high and narrow . . . "

Prison food, Harmand noted, could hardly have been expected to benefit the dauphin's worsening condition: "His dinner was composed of a blackish soup with a few lentils floating on the surface, served in an earthenware porringer; on a plate of the same crockery was a small piece of very tough-looking boiled beef; a second plate contained more lentils, and on a third plate were six chestnuts, more burnt than baked; a pewter spoon and fork were placed by the side of the porringer; the commissaries told us that the *Conseil de la Commune* had ordered that the child was on no account to be allowed to use a knife; there was no wine."

This last was hardly trivial. No wine meant no beverage at all with his meal. Again the commissaries insisted that they were only following orders.

The inspector quickly issued new orders, specifying changes in the regimen to improve both the boy's health and his state of mind. For, as he also noted of the occasion, "his expression did not alter for a single moment; there was not the slightest trace of any emotion . . . it was just as if we were not there."

But Harmand had to leave Paris a short time later on an undisclosed mission, and he was never able to see that his new orders were carried out. Presumably they were not. For, less than six months later, the youngster was pronounced dead.

However, the secrecy of those last months left room for doubt. No sooner was the boy's body laid to rest than people began to say he had not died of neglect but that he was murdered, instead—by poison, starvation, or outright physical assault. Many noted that, only the week before, a prominent surgeon named Desault had died suddenly and under mysterious circumstances.

It was this Dr. Desault who had been summoned in May, 1795, to treat the ailing dauphin. And it was Desault's own widow who hinted of the doctor's refusal to take part in some irregular practice regarding his patient. Hence, the inference of the mob: If he would not kill, he must himself be killed to preserve the good name of the Revolution!

Others, however, claimed that the dauphin had not died at all. He had, they said, been rescued from the Temple by royalist sympathizers and another child substituted for him in the cell. Little enough, after all, had been seen of the dauphin once the tutor Simon made his exit. As for Desault, it was possible that he had been killed by royalists, not revolutionists, because he recognized the switch and thus jeopardized their carefully laid plans for Louis Charles' escape.

The language of the official autopsy did nothing to clear up doubts. The dauphin, it was reported, had died "from a scrofulous affection [tuberculosis] of long standing."

An article in the December, 1799 issue of *European Magazine* vigorously joined in "denial that this interesting child had a scrofulous disease. Neither the House of Bourbon, nor that of Austria, were afflicted with that malady; the babe could not have contracted it. When this bulletin arrived in England, with the concomitant report that the young sufferer had been poisoned by the Committee of Safety, some very extraordinary circumstances occurred or transpired.

"All the world believed the young King to have been murdered. The British Cabinet, with no other opinion, ordered the bulletin to be examined by a physician of the very first reputation. This gentleman reported to the King's Council that the young King could not have died of the cause assigned in the bulletin. The case was fictitious, and the consequence would not have followed from the premises, even if they had been true."

Nor did doctors present at the inquest necessarily support the authenticity of the death certificate. Indeed, they pointedly asserted that their only function was to examine the corpse and render judgment as to probable cause of death. They were not called upon to identify the corpse!

Rumors spread and gained wide support. For one reason or another, people began to discount the murder theory. Speculation centered on the boy's escape. By 1814, even Simien Despréaux, official historian of the restored monarchy under Louis XVIII (younger brother of the late King Louis XVI), recorded that Louis Charles had not only survived imprisonment but was still alive. He could not, however, say where or in what circumstances.

Finally, in 1846, the coffin was exhumed and the skeleton

examined to establish the identity. But this served only to compound the mystery. For, although the body was certainly small enough to have been that of the dauphin, the limbs seemed much too long for that body. They seemed more like those of a boy in his middle to late teens. And the skull bore a wisdom tooth already cut.

Yet, if the dauphin had escaped—if, as Despréaux says, he was still alive at the time of the restoration—why had he himself not ascended to the throne? He would have been officially recognized as Louis XVII.

Several answers have been suggested. The first, of course, is that his ambitious uncle prevented the succession by force or by persuasion. The latter might not have been so difficult, inasmuch as the delicate dauphin had been so greatly weakened by his confinement. Indeed, he may well have been physically inadequate to bear the burdens of the crown. Ultimately, it must also be considered that poor Louis Charles, weak or strong, might have by then become wholly disenchanted with the notion of responsibility for a kingdom —or fed up with the ingratitude of its subjects.

Since that time, however, some forty pretenders have laid claim to the dauphin's title. Most were quickly and easily discredited. A few were not.

At least one man linked with Louis Charles never made the claim himself, though later generations questioned the curious coincidences of birth. This was John James Audubon, celebrated artist and naturalist, whose studies of North American birds brought him fame and fortune in his own right.

According to official records, Audubon was the illegitimate son of a French naval officer who had business dealings with revolutionists in both France and America. He was born in Les Cayes, Santo Domingo (now in Haiti), on April 26, 1785.

Louis Charles, it should be noted, was born on March 27, 1785.

There was no certificate of Audubon's birth, however. There was only a doctor's bill stating date and fee but neglecting to mention even the mother's name. The bill was nonetheless accepted as proof of birth when the elder Audubon legally adopted the boy. This was on March 7, 1794—less than two months after Antoine Simon left the Temple's royal prisoner to his dark and mysterious seclusion!

On a visit to Paris in 1828, Audubon wrote to his wife in Kentucky a letter full of anguish and enigma:

> I see my father before me with his proud eagle's eye frowning on me as if I had leaped over the abyss. . . . I must try to bury the dreadful past in oblivion. Peaceful woods, to you I must return, and under your dark shades, consecrate my days to the only blessing left me on this earth, that of admiring the works of a Creator who knows who I am, and will repay me for my torments here below.
>
> What might this day have been, if known here? Patient, silent, bashful, and yet powerful of physique and of mind, dressed as a common man, I walk the streets! I bow! I ask permission to do this or that! I follow the publication of a work on natural history that has apparently absorbed my whole knowing life, *I, who should command all!*

Coincidences notwithstanding, the Audubon family never advanced more than tentative claim to noble ancestry. It was a matter of inference, not insistence.

Somewhat more outspoken was the claim of another American, a missionary named Eleazar Williams. The adopted son of a half-breed Iroquois chief, Williams was raised in the Lake George area of upper New York State. Supposedly, his real identity was unknown even to himself.

"You must imagine," Williams once said of himself, "a child who, as far as he knows anything, was an idiot. His mind is a blank until thirteen or fourteen years of age. He was destitute even of consciousness that can be remembered until that period. He was bathing in Lake George among a group of Indian boys. He clambered with the fearlessness of idiocy to the top of a high rock. He plunged head-foremost into the water. He was taken up insensible and laid in an Indian hut. He was brought to life. There was the blue sky, there were the mountains, there were the waters. That was the first I knew of life."

The past came to him, he said, in the person of the Prince de Joinville, son of Louis XVIII. Joinville was visiting in the area during the fall of 1841. He met Williams on a boat trip from Buffalo to Green Bay.

According to Williams, the prince recognized him at once, embraced him, and entrusted to him the secret of his regal birth. Later, at a hotel in Green Bay, the prince showed him a document confirming the assertion. If Williams would sign the document, which acknowledged his own abdication of the throne, he would be rewarded with a huge estate in either France or America, as he preferred. But Williams refused to sign.

Such was the character of the missionary's reputation that no historian has ever seen fit to question the sincerity of his belief in the story. The most that has been suggested is that he was the victim of a practical joke, a trifling but cruel diversion employed by the prince to relieve the boredom of a long trip.

Joinville, of course, denied the story. He did, however, admit freely to having met the missionary on a boat trip. He remembered conversing with him at length and even proposing the subsequent exchange of letters and documents on the history of French establishments in America.

"All the rest," he argued, "all which treats of the revelation which the Prince made to Mr. Williams, of the mystery of his birth, all which concerns the pretended personage of Louis XVII., is from one end to the other a work of the imagination, a fable woven wholesale, a speculation upon the public credulity."

It is unlikely, to say the least, that the king's own son would have deliberately sought out the rightful heir to his father's throne. That he would have proceeded at once, not only to inform the stranger of his rights but to ask him to renounce those rights as well, is incredible.

Yet, the romantic in Eleazar Williams ran strong. Maybe it got the better of him in the end. For he persisted throughout the last seventeen years of his life in the belief that it was he, to use Audubon's curious phrase, "who should command all."

The headstone of Williams' grave in Hogansburg, New York, bears only his name and the date of his death. The details of his birth have been omitted.

However, in Gleize, France, there is another headstone with the far more imposing inscription:

CI-GIT
Louis-Charles de France
Fils de Louis XVI. et de Marie-Antoinette
Né à Versailles le 27 Mars, 1785,
Mort à Gleize le 10 Août, 1853

This is the gravesite of one Comte de Richemont, a handsome, flamboyant man also of unknown birth, who in his lifetime used nearly a dozen aliases and was probably as bold an impostor as history has ever known. His actions remind one of Danton's own prescription for revolutionary success: "Audacity, audacity, and more audacity."

He would not deign to prove his identity as Louis Charles. Instead, he shifted that burden to the crown. If not Louis Charles, he asked, then who am I? It was a public challenge.

At first he petitioned Louis XVIII only for recognition, disavowing any interest in the throne. He was rejected out of hand. Worse yet, he was dismissed as a worthless fraud. It was a public humiliation, and it so enraged Richemont that he issued a formal protest to all European heads of state asserting his royal birth and declaring that the present king of France had literally stolen the throne from him.

Louis wasted no time in retaliating. He ordered the pretender arrested at once, leaving him to languish some seven years in prison. Still Richemont would not give up. Upon his release, in 1832, he took up the protest where he had left off. Again he was packed off to jail—this time for fourteen months before he was finally brought to trial.

His personal charm was winning; yet his case proved anything but popular. In all of France he could not find a single lawyer to plead it for him. Sentenced to twelve years, he managed to escape a few months after the trial and did not return to France until the general amnesty of 1840.

Richemont died in 1853, and the offending headstone in Gleize was shortly thereafter turned to face the wall of the church it abutted. A less pretentious epitaph was engraved on the reverse side. Somehow the two-faced stone still seems a most fitting monument to the man's career.

Not the least colorful episode of that career was the interruption of his trial in 1834 by the celebrated "man in black." The intruder was a tall, distinguished-looking man with white hair and uniformly black attire. He entered in the midst of court proceedings and delivered to the judge an enormous document sealed with the arms of France. He was an emissary of Louis XVII, he said, and he had come to protest the protests of the pretender Richemont.

The Louis XVII he represented was, in fact, a German clockmaker named Karl Wilhelm Naundorff. And of all the claimants to the dauphin's title, it is this Naundorff who must be taken most seriously.

He must be taken seriously if only because he was so convincing at the time. He quickly gained widespread allegiance and financial support. So popular was his cause, in fact, that for a time it posed a very real threat to the governing power of Louis XVIII. And, considering the nearly incredible account of the years prior to his return to Paris, this was no mean accomplishment.

His story of escape from the Temple, for example, was awkward at best. It was rather like a game of "musical cells," involving as it did the complex substitution of many children in various parts of the Temple during the year 1795.

The escape was followed by a series of arrests that obliged him to spend, in all, seventeen of the next twenty-four years in prison. Causes of such harassment were never explained. But Naundorff carefully planted the suspicion that some mysterious "they" had arranged it all.

In 1820, however, he turned up in a Berlin court on the very well explained, if mundane, charge of counterfeiting—of having, as he later put it, "endeavored to circulate false coin." He was acquitted and went back to working for a living at his old trade. And it was not until 1833 that he finally made it to Paris, where he set out to prove his real identity.

He did an impressive job. For, whereas Richemont had offered only bald assertions, Naundorff at least presented evidence of his claim to fame. This won him important backing at the outset.

First of all, he looked like a Bourbon—very much as Louis Charles might have looked at his age. This was eagerly attested by the dauphin's childhood nurse, Madame de Rambaud. How she cherished her memories of the dauphin during those days before the Revolution! How well she remembered the details of his appearance, scars and birthmarks and all! Naundorff fit her description almost to a tee.

Moreover, he knew his facts. She questioned him at length about childhood episodes, and was well satisfied with his answers.

At one point, to test him further, she showed him the blue coat he'd worn on a special occasion in Paris as a boy; she had saved it as a memento. No, he corrected her, he had worn that particular coat only on the palace grounds at Versailles and never in the city.

He was right, she agreed. The coat was never worn in Paris.

She took him to Prague to see the Duchesse d'Angoulême, the dauphin's sister, who by then had married the new king's son and her own cousin. For reasons never stated, the duchess declined to receive him. And, in 1836, Naundorff filed suit against her for recovery of property belonging to Louis Charles.

At that point, he was arrested without charge and deported.

Why the government never brought him to trial was not officially explained. Naundorff's supporters immediately charged that the king could not risk a public hearing at which real evidence and identification might be presented. Richemont, after all, had received swift justice.

Much was made, too, of a visionary named Thomas Ignace Martin. Twenty years earlier, Martin had contributed immensely to the dauphin legend with a report to the king that he, Louis XVIII, should hand over his throne to its rightful heir. Louis Charles, he said, was still alive and still fit to serve. Curiously, the king took no offense at the suggestion, which was made long before the writings of Despréaux were disclosed. He even offered the seer a sum of money for his trouble.

Martin left Versailles unheeded, and that was the end of that. He had nothing more to say on the subject for fully two decades. Yet, as soon as Naundorff appeared in Paris, Martin positively and publicly identified him as the dauphin. A short time later, he was murdered.

Naundorff himself was nearly killed when two men jumped and knifed him as he walked along the Paris streets one night in January, 1834. "He was," wrote the Curate of Saint Arnoult, Abbé Appert, in a letter to a friend, "attacked and received six strokes from a dagger, but was miraculously saved. The surgeon certified that the dagger had stopped within a half line of the heart; you are aware that five of the blows were parried by a medal of our Lord and the Holy Virgin, which was pierced, and by his beads and crucifix, which were broken to pieces."

A second attempt was made to assassinate him during his brief exile in London. These incidents added greatly to the romantic luster of his claim. But they did not encourage Naundorff in the pursuit of it.

Settled at last in the Netherlands, Naundorff spent his remaining years quietly engaged in mechanical occupations. In addition to the clockmaking and repair work that had been his principal source of income before 1834, he worked on designs and models of a new projectile weapon that he eventually sold to the Dutch war ministry.

He died at Delft in 1845 and was buried under a tombstone inscribed, like Richemont's:

Ici Répose
LOUIS XVII.
Charles-Louis, Duc de Normandie,
Roi de France et de Navarre,
Né à Versailles le 27 Mars, 1785,
Décédé à Delft le 10 Août, 1845.

Unlike Richemont's, however, the stone covering the Naundorff grave was left untouched. And, in 1863, the States-General of the Netherlands went so far as to authorize Naundorff's son to assume the name "de Bourbon." Fifty years later, in November, 1913, when a noted journalist disputed the family's right to the name, a French court not only upheld the validity of the judgment of the Dutch government but also fined the writer 500 francs for libel!

One thing the rivals Richemont and Naundorff shared, strangely enough, was their date of death. Both died on August 10, with Richemont surviving Naundorff by eight years. It is perhaps worth noting that August 10 was also the date on which, in 1792, the dauphin was originally committed with his family to imprisonment in the Temple.

And that, after all, is where the story really began.

Photograph of the Grand Duchess Anastasia from *Gestalten Von Letzten Zarenhof* by Louise Reibnitz-Maltzan.— *Photograph courtesy Slavonic Division, The New York Public Library, Astor, Lenox and Tilden Foundations.*

LAST
OF
THE
ROMANOVS

---

the
legend
of
Grand
Duchess Anastasia . . .

REVOLUTION HAD ENDED. The violence of counterrevolution was already under way.

A surprisingly strong Czech Legion captured the all-important Trans-Siberian Railway from Chelyabinsk to Vladivostok. White Russian armies drove westward from Siberia through the Ural Mountains.

There in the town of Ekaterinburg (now Sverdlovsk), the ousted Czar Nicholas II was held prisoner by the newly established Bolshevik regime. He and his family were quartered in the house of an engineer, N. N. Ipatiev, at the top of a hill overlooking the city. They had lived there under heavy guard since late May, despite the best efforts of German and English diplomacy to gain their freedom.

But their future posed an anxious problem for local authorities. If released, the family would form a natural rallying point for counterrevolutionary forces at home and abroad. Yet every moment of their imprisonment bore with it the threat of their escape. Now, with enemy armies advancing on the town, that threat was more pressing than ever.

On July 16, 1918, the Ekaterinburg soviet called for execution of the entire royal assemblage. This included not only the czar and his wife but also their only son and erstwhile heir, Alexei Nicholaievitch, their four daughters—Olga, Maria, Tatiana, and Anastasia—three servants, and the czar's personal physician, Dr. Eugene Botkin.

Later, near midnight, the prisoners were roused from sleep by soldiers and herded into the cellar. A local commissar came in and hastily read a one-line death warrant. Then he drew his revolver and shot the czar through the head.

His men took their cue at once, spraying the room with gunfire. Their victims fell quietly. The soldiers moved among the bodies, bayoneting them and smashing their heads with rifle butts. Any sign of life was worth another shot. Then the corpses were carried off into the night, taken to a mining town nearby, and dropped into a pit. Finally, they were doused with sulphuric acid to char the remains beyond recognition.

Such was the pathetic downfall of the Romanovs, a dynasty, Russia's ruling family for more than 300 years. But the legends surrounding them had just begun.

Everywhere there were rumors that one member of the family had miraculously escaped. Some said it was Alexei, others one of his sisters. Speculation centered heavily on two of the younger girls, Tatiana and Anastasia.

Then, in February, 1920, a policeman in Berlin spotted a young woman leaping from a bridge across the Landwehr Canal. He jumped in after her, pulled her from the icy waters, and rushed her to nearby Elizabeth Hospital. This act of heroism was to spawn one of the most dramatic controversies of the twentieth century—"a historical mystery," as it was later characterized by a Berlin police inspector named Albert Grünberg, "comparable to that of the Man in the Iron Mask."

The woman was taken to Dalldorf Sanitarium, where she spent the next two years. The admitting physician noted in his records that she apparently suffered from partial amnesia and paranoid delusions. He estimated her age at about twenty.

At Dalldorf, the frail young woman was recognized by a fellow patient, Klara Marie Peuthert. As soon as she was released, Frau Peuthert hurried off to visit Baron Arthur von Kleist with the news that she had found Tatiana, second daughter of Czar Nicholas. Kleist, she understood, was well known in Russian emigré circles and could produce the witnesses to corroborate her discovery.

Unfortunately, the first witness Kleist called upon was the Baroness Isa Buxhoeveden, former lady-in-waiting to the czar's wife and empress, Alexandra Fyodorovna. The baroness needed only a glance to tell her the Dalldorf patient could not be Tatiana; for Tatiana had been the tallest of the four daughters, and this woman was, in fact, quite short.

Frau Peuthert readily acknowledged her mistake. It was not Tatiana, of course. It was Anastasia, the czar's youngest daughter. Eventually, the woman was induced to tell the story of her "rescue."

Among the guards at the Ipatiev house, she said, were two brothers, Alexander and Sergei Tchaikovsky. Early in the morning of July 17, while other members of the imperial family were being carted off to their common burial in a mining pit, one of the brothers noticed some life remaining in the young woman's body. Whether moved by a spark of compassion or some lingering loyalty to the Romanovs, the two men sneaked her off to one side and hid her from the other soldiers. Later, while those others slept, they took her to a nearby farmhouse for safekeeping. And there they spent the night. Next day, they began a grueling journey to the Rumanian border.

The roads were rough, the trip long. In all, it was about 1,500 miles. The three travelers changed horses often, even bought new carts when the wheels of the old ones became worn. Their money came from the sale of some jewelry the czarina had sewn in the lining of Anastasia's dress—as she had in the clothes of all her children. By winter, they had made it safely to Bucharest.

The woman herself had few sure memories of the trek. She suffered both the physical wounds and the emotional traumata of that July night in the cellar of the Ipatiev house. And these had rendered her into a prolonged state of shock, or "nervous fever" as she called it. She remembered her illness, the bumpy roads they traveled, the experience of sexual intercourse with Alexander—but only vaguely.

In Bucharest, she bore her rescuer a son and was married in a Rumanian church. They lived together with Alexander's brother, Sergei, until the following summer, when Alexander was mysteriously assassinated. She remembered having left the house for his funeral. And she had some hazy recollection that their baby was taken from her soon afterward and placed in an orphanage.

Presumably fleeing Bolshevik assassins, she and Sergei hastily moved on. They crossed the German border and made their way safely to Berlin. There they took rooms in a cheap hotel.

Night fell, but Anna Tchaikovsky could not sleep. She paced the floor of her room, then went out to seek Sergei's company. But the guardian brother-in-law was gone, had disappeared, deserted her there in that foreign city.

Desperate and bewildered, she roamed the streets that night. She walked through a park until she came upon a canal bridge. She leaned over the side of the bridge and gazed for a while at the mist across the water. Then she jumped.

From that point on, Inspector Grünberg was in charge of her case. He believed her story, even took her into his home some time after she had left Dalldorf. It was at his instigation that she was visited by the Princess Irene. The princess was Anastasia's godmother and an aunt on her mother's side.

This was in August, 1922. Irene had come from Rumania to confirm or deny the identity of a girl she had not seen for ten years.

Their reunion, however, was anything but cordial. Instead, the princess was greeted with a hysterical outburst that led her to doubt that this could possibly be the lovable, warm-hearted little Anastasia she remembered.

Yet the young girl definitely looked the part.

"The hair, forehead, and eyes are Anastasia's," Irene observed, "but the mouth and chin are not." After some deliberation, she could only conclude: "I cannot say that it isn't her."

Similarly, the Crown Princess Cecilie of Germany was unable to make positive identification. She was introduced by Grünberg shortly after the episode with Irene; and she, too, drew a cold response from the girl who said she was her distant cousin.

"It was virtually impossible to communicate with the young person," she later declared. "She remained completely silent, either from obstinacy or because she was completely bewildered, I could not decide which."

The crown princess also noted, however, that she had been "struck at first glance by the young person's resemblance to the czar's mother and the czar himself."

Indeed, from the moment Klara Peuthert first saw her at Dalldorf, that family likeness had been the mainstay of the Tchaikovsky woman's case for recognition as the Grand Duchess Anastasia. Even those who disputed the identity had to admit the resemblance. Pierre Gilliard, a tutor employed by the czar for his children, felt certain the young woman in question was not the Anastasia he had known and taught. Still, he agreed that there were similarities of appearance.

These similarities more strongly impressed his wife, Shura, the children's governess.

"With my reason," she confided to the Danish Ambassador, Herluf Zahle, "I cannot grasp that it might be Anastasia, although my heart tells me it *is* she. And as I have grown up in a religion which teaches me to follow my heart rather than my reason, I cannot forsake this unhappy child."

The ambassador himself had been dispatched by Anastasia's Aunt Olga, her father's youngest sister, who had escaped to Copenhagen after the revolution. "He had never met my niece," Olga later told her biographer, Ian Vorres, "but he was a scholar, and the whole story seemed to him the greatest historical puzzle of the century, and he was determined to solve it."

Zahle's report strongly supported Mrs. Tchaikovsky's claim to be the Grand Duchess Anastasia. Not only did she look so much like photographs of the girl he had seen in family albums, but she also bore specific identity marks. One finger of her left hand had been badly injured, just as had Anastasia's, by the slamming of a car door—an incident, by the way, that seems to have been forgotten by the rest of the family until the Tchaikovsky woman herself mentioned it. There was a scar on her right shoulder, where Anastasia had had a mole cauterized as a child. Her feet were marred by bunions, worse on the right foot than on the left, just as Anastasia had such a deformity. She suffered from a bad case of bone tuberculosis, a condition common among the Romanovs. Finally, the young woman referred to her Aunt Olga's having called her years earlier by the pet name "Shvipsik"; this was a name known to only a few members of the family and palace staff.

But the young woman in question also had several strikes against her. In the years following the revolution, fantastic rumors of survival had brought forth a host of impostors all over Europe and abroad, each claiming to be one or another of the children of Russia's imperial family. Response among the related royal households of Germany and Denmark was naturally suspicious.

Then, too, Mrs. Tchaikovsky's claims were remarkably unsupported by document or testimony. Too many questions remained unanswered.

Why, for one thing, had she waited so long in claiming her right to the title? And why was she so uncooperative, even hysterical and hostile, when examined by those who might have confirmed her claim? Why could Grünberg find no trace of a Sergei Tchaikovsky anywhere in Germany or Rumania? Why, for that matter, could he not find an orphanage-held child who might conceivably have been hers? How did it happen that she was so fluent in German but hardly spoke Russian, English, and French? After all, she had been trained in these latter languages as a child—but never in German.

It was perhaps the language question that cast the gravest doubt on her claim.

"I readily admit that a ghastly horror experienced in one's youth can work havoc with one's memory," the Grand Duchess Olga subsequently remarked, "but I have never heard of any ghastly experience endowing anyone with a knowledge they had not had before it happened. My nieces knew no German at all."

In 1927, a private detective named Martin Knopf came up with an interesting and plausible theory to account for this discrepancy. Mrs. Tchaikovsky, he said, was no grand duchess at all—not even Russian, in fact, but a Polish peasant girl who had disappeared from her Berlin apartment on February 15, 1920. This girl, Franziska Schanzkovsky, also had a family history of bone tuberculosis as well as a medical record of foot disorders and the removal of a birthmark on her right shoulder. More important, her native Polish was a language closely akin to Russian; and she might easily have been able to understand the latter without being able to speak it comfortably.

Knopf produced Doris Wingender to back up his charges. This woman was the daughter of Franziska's landlady in Berlin, and she readily concurred that Mrs. Tchaikovsky and her mother's missing tenant were one and the same person.

However, Franziska's brother, Felix, wasn't so sure. He would say only that the two women looked alike, nothing more. (Eleven years later, Franziska's two sisters likewise refused to identify Mrs. Tchaikovsky.)

Ostensibly, Knopf was working on the case as an investigator for the evening newspaper *Nachtausgabe*. But there was—and has been ever since—strong speculation that he actually represented the House of Hesse-Darmstadt, a noble German family related by marriage to the Romanovs.

Mrs. Tchaikovsky had already made for herself an unrelenting foe of the Grand Duke Ernst Ludwig von Hesse-Darmstadt. In the course of a seemingly casual conversation, she remarked that she had seen her "Uncle Ernie" in Saint Petersburg as recently as 1916. Naturally, he hotly denied the allegation. For Germany and Russia were at war in 1916, and any such visit could only have been a mission to seek peace. His fellow Germans, especially the more nationalistic among them, would never have forgiven such a mission. Instead, they might well have construed it as an attempt to sell out the fatherland.

Yet, testimony at legal hearings later supported Mrs. Tchaikovsky's contention. A former colonel in the Russian guards regiment remembered having seen the Grand Duke in Finland with one of the czar's high-ranking officers, a Colonel Mordvinov: "When Mordvinov saw I had recognized the Grand Duke, he asked me to make no sign of this and to keep quiet about it. He told me the Empress' brother was traveling incognito, under the name of a Prince Thurn-and-Taxis."

And the Crown Princess Cecilie of Germany, who had earlier been so impressed by the Romanov look of the woman claiming to be Anastasia, declared on oath in 1953: "If the view is still held today that such a visit never took place, I can assert from personal knowledge—the source is my late father-in-law—that our circles knew about it even at the time. So in my opinion, by making such a statement (which I only heard of much later), Mrs. A. T. was giving strong evidence that at least she had intimate knowledge of high politics and the most secret dealings of the Imperial family."

Another bit of "intimate knowledge" figured largely in Anna Tchaikovsky's quarrel with the Hesse-Darmstadts. This was her statement to Ambassador Zahle that the czar had left some 20 million rubles on deposit for his daughters either with the Bank of England or with one of the private banks in England. What Nicholas intended for his son and heir, Alexis, was not made clear; but the alleged sum put aside for the four girls was large enough. Anastasia's share alone would have been worth perhaps 6 or 7 million dollars—

four times that amount, of course, once she was recognized as the sole heiress. With Anastasia out of the picture, however, the money would go to the few remaining Romanovs in exile and to the Hesse-Darmstadt family in Germany.

To this day the money has never been found. But, in 1933, the Berlin Civil Court granted other members of the two families a document of inheritance, which, while it covered Russian property in Germany only, put an official stamp on the assertion that all of the czar's immediate family had been murdered and that the woman Anna Tchaikovsky was nothing more than an impostor.

This was the beginning of a legal battle that has been waged ever since. As late as 1970, the case was still in the courts—on the basis of a 1937 application for cancellation of that document. The burden of proof, by then, was entirely Mrs. Tchaikovsky's—to prove that she *was* the grand duchess and that she *had* been miraculously spared the slaughter of that night in the Ipatiev house.

After more than fifty years, it was a nearly impossible burden. Witnesses who might have helped were dead, papers lost or destroyed.

One of those witnesses was Gleb Botkin, son of Czar Nicholas' personal physician. He and Anastasia were childhood friends, had played together in the palace and even shared for a time the imperial family's exile. A favorite pastime, he recalled, was to caricature various men and women about the palace as animallike creatures. He would do the drawings in his room sometimes and smuggle them out to Anastasia and her sisters for their amusement.

He showed a few of these drawings to Mrs. Tchaikovsky when he met her in 1927, and she identified them immediately. This knowledge, together with her strong physical resemblance to the girl he had known, convinced him "without the shadow of doubt" that she was Anastasia.

A more recent supporter is Dr. John E. Manahan, a former professor of history who was active throughout the 1960s trying to establish the woman's identity. Dr. Manahan's concern was largely academic, though, inasmuch as he and the woman in question only met for the first time in July, 1968. But a friendship fast developed between them; and the two were married in Charlottesville, Virginia, in December of the same year.

Today, however, there is little real hope for recognition. The most recent appeal to the West German Supreme Court was rejected in February, 1970; and, although much was subsequently made of the fact that the court's ruling was based not on the question of identity but on a lower court's procedures, the most that history is likely ever to allow was echoed in the words of Princess Irene: "I cannot say that it isn't her."

In any event, the woman has spent her entire adult life as Anastasia, Grand Duchess of Imperial Russia. If she has spent it vainly seeking to right the wrongs of the past, she has done so valiantly. If, on the other hand, she has lived it as a fraud, she has done so well enough never to have been disproved.

The facts of the case have long since been obscured. And only the legend remains.

The baptism of Virginia Dare from *The Lost Colony*, drama presented each summer at Waterside Theatre, Fort Raleigh National Historic Site, near Manteo, North Carolina.—Photograph taken from *Paradise Preserved*, copyright 1965 by Roanoke Island Historical Association.

CROATOAN

---

*the
lost
colony
of
Roanoke Island ...*

THE GOVERNOR HAD been gone three years. Yet no one came to meet him when he landed. Indeed, there seemed to be no one left on Roanoke Island at all. There was only that simple, enigmatic greeting: CRO.

Just the letters, nothing more. They were carved into the trunk of a tree along his path. Further on, another tree bore the fuller inscription: CROATOAN.

Otherwise, there was nothing. There was no sign of slaughter, no sign of any struggle. Weeds had long since covered the ground where buildings once stood. The buildings had been dismantled. Supplies were gone. And all the settlers had vanished.

There had been 120 of them, including Governor John White's own daughter and her infant child. They had settled there in the late summer of 1587 after two unsuccessful attempts by others to stake an English claim along the outer banks of what is now North Carolina.

Or, more correctly, they were deposited there by an unconcerned ship's captain.

No one knows just where the new governor actually hoped to settle his band. Some think he wanted to go farther north, perhaps along Chesapeake Bay. In any case, Roanoke Island was definitely not the place he had in mind. It had already borne too many failures.

But the captain of their ships protested. He had contracted with Sir Walter Raleigh to transport them across the ocean and into this vicinity. That was all. He had already lost too much time in being thus diverted from his regular West Indies trade. He was growing impatient to return to London for more profitable cargo.

So, after the party was taken ashore to search for remains of a previous expedition, the captain ordered his sailors to return to ship. And the colonists were virtually abandoned to their fate.

White's party differed fundamentally from their predecessors. These people had come to stay. They were attempting to found the first permanent English colony in America.

There were seventeen women and half a dozen children among them. The birth of another child shortly after their arrival was duly noted in White's journal on August 18:

> . . . Eleanor, daughter to the governor, and wife to Ananias Dare, one of the assistants, was delivered of a daughter in Roanoak, and the same was christened there the Sunday following, and because this child was the first christian born in Virginia, she was named Virginia.

It was the queen herself who had named the region, in which she gave Raleigh a "patent" to any discoveries that might be made there. She called the land "Virginia," presumably in tribute to her own maiden state. Now it remained for the romance of American history to make a legend of the name Virginia Dare.

White's settlement, however, had more than women and children to distinguish it from any other. Because it was meant to be a permanent colony, it was the first to have made clear-cut arrangements for colonial government. White, of course, had been appointed by Raleigh. The good knight also chose twelve "assistants," among them Ananias Dare, to serve with White as a kind of town council. For guidelines he drew up a charter of the colony's purposes and outlined basic statutes.

But the governor's tenure was short-lived. He remained with the settlers on Roanoke Island no more than thirty-six days.

During that time, all of them began to realize how ill-prepared they really were. In the first place, the lands were not nearly as rich as they had imagined; and the supplies and food they had brought with them were inadequate. Bare sustenance would mean hard work. And their very survival was ever threatened by their vulnerability to Indian attack.

White's assistants asked that he return for aid. The ships that had brought them there were still at anchor, awaiting propitious winds and tides. He could sail for England with them, obtain all the supplies they might need, and still be back before the worst of winter was upon them.

But the governor refused. His place was with the people he had brought so far from home. Whatever hardship they faced, he would face with them.

The point was pressed at a meeting of all the colonists. The governor could best serve their interests, they claimed, not by staying with them but by going back on their behalf.

Again White declined, but only briefly. And, on August 27, he departed with the fleet.

It was not an easy parting. For among those he left behind were his daughter, Eleanor, and his nine-day-old grandchild, Virginia.

It was the last he would ever see of them.

White had expected to be gone only a few months at the most. Instead, he was abroad three years. Not only was the return crossing slowed by late-summer storms, but when at last he was safely docked in England he found his mission brought to a complete halt. The mother country was busy preparing for war with Spain. The growing Spanish Armada had come to rule the Atlantic, and suddenly the threat of invasion was the talk of London. No one had time for Roanoke Island, least of all Raleigh. He was now a leading member of the council of war.

By April, White had prevailed on Raleigh's former commercial interests to obtain the use of a small fleet for the settlers' relief. He began loading immediately. But before he could set sail, a state of emergency was declared throughout the country. Every ship was impressed for military action. And White had to surrender those few ships without ever having had a chance to use them.

He did succeed, however, in acquiring other vessels. These were much smaller craft, too small to be taken for battle. Still, they were better than nothing; and, on April 22, he set out at last for the Carolina coast.

Unfortunately, the sailors he'd hired were not very interested in the Carolina coast. They were spoiling for a fight. Indeed, they went out of their way to search for enemy vessels. And their little ships were badly damaged in the encounters that ensued—so much so that they had to return home before more than a fraction of the voyage had been completed.

England's subsequent victory over the Armada was her glory. But it was a sad glory for the displaced governor of Roanoke Island. Raleigh's personal fortune had been greatly reduced by the cost of the effort, and no other benefactors could be found to finance the expedition. Not until March, 1590, was Raleigh again able to provide for White's return.

He secured the service of a three-vessel fleet under the command of one John Watts. And he arranged for it to take on not just cargo for the settlers on Roanoke Island but still more people who would settle there with them. Once more, however, fate played against them.

Watts was first and foremost a trader. If he made the trip, he would make it only by way of the West Indies. That route offered prospects for both lucrative trading and the capture of Spanish prizes of war. Obviously, more space was needed on board for such contingencies.

"I was," White later wrote to a friend, "by the owner and commander of the ships, denied to have any passengers, or any thing else transported in any of the said ships, saving only myself and my chest; no, not so much as a boy to attend upon me. . . . I could have no opportunity to go unto Sir Walter Raleigh with complaint: for the ships, being then all in readiness to go to the sea, would have departed before I could have made my return. Thus, both governors, masters and sailors, regarding very small the good of their countrymen in Virginia, determined nothing less than to touch at those places, but wholly disposed themselves to seek after purchase and spoils, spending so much time therein, that summer was spent before we arrived at Virginia."

A final touch was added to the misfortune with the drowning of four sailors in the rough waters that almost kept them from landing at all. Indeed, it was only by the captain's intervention that the remaining crew were persuaded not to abandon the task. They laid anchor and went in with White to seek the settlers out.

In vain they searched. The colonists were gone, and scarcely a trace of them remained. There were no bodies; there were no signs of battle. The ground was covered over with high grass and weeds. The closest White or any member of the searching party came to contact with human life was the discovery of a fresh set of footprints—probably those of an Indian hunter—in sand near the northern tip of the island.

On a sandy bank nearby they came upon a tree that had been stripped of its bark. On it were carved those curious letters: CRO.

What did it mean? Was it a message left for White by his colonists? Was it a warning? A signal of distress?

"And having well considered of this," White later recorded, "we passed toward the place where they were left in sundry houses, but we found the houses taken down and the place very strongly enclosed, with a high palisado of great trees, with curtains and flankers very fort-like, and one of the chief trees or posts at the right side of the entrance had the bark taken off, and five feet from the ground in fair capital letters was graven CROATOAN without any cross or sign of distress; this done, we entered the palisado, where we found many bars of iron, two pigs of lead, four iron-fowlers, iron sacker-shot, and such like heavy things thrown here and there, almost overgrown with grass and weeds. From thence, we went along the water side, towards the point of the creek to see if we could find any of their boats or pinnace, but we could perceive no sign of them nor any of the last falcons or small ordinance which were left with them at my departure from them."

What, then, did happen to the men and women of Roanoke Island? The disappearance remains a mystery to this day. Their fate can only be surmised.

"One of the most plausible theories—though seldom advanced—is that the colonists, finally despairing of relief, sailed for England in a boat which had been left with them by White in 1587 and were lost at sea." So says the North Carolina historian Hugh T. Lefler.

Other theories center on the vulnerability of the colonists to attack. Some say they were wiped out by Spanish troops. Indeed, contemporary documents assembled by David B. Quinn, professor of history at the University of Wales, reveal plans for a military expedition from Spain to "liquidate" the colony of Roanoke Island and establish a settlement farther north to extend Spanish control of America's east coast. (Posts had already been built on the Florida shore.) But these plans were changed at the last minute, says Quinn, to make ships available for transporting recently garnered treasures from the New World.

"The North American expedition, first postponed, was then abandoned," he contends, "so that when John White found, in July 1590, that the third colony had disappeared, it had not, at least, been overwhelmed by the Spaniards."

Still others think an Indian attack more likely, the signs CRO and CROATOAN being the last, desperate act of those beleaguered colonists to name their assassins. But the Croatoan (or Hatteras) had always been among the most friendly of the Indian tribes. They lived on a neighboring island, now called Hatteras Island; and, from the start, they had actually encouraged the Roanoke settlement. They brought food and even offered assistance in making camp. It seems far more likely to many scholars that, if the signs meant anything at all, they were carved to indicate the people with whom the colonists had taken refuge after being attacked by a savage, nomadic tribe of Indians in the region.

"A farther Confirmation of this we have from the Hatteras Indians," wrote the historian John Lawson in 1709, "who either then lived on Ronoak-Island or much frequented it. These tell us, that several of their Ancestors were white People, and could talk in a Book, as we do; the Truth of which is confirmed by grey Eyes [a European, not an Indian characteristic] being found frequently amongst these Indians, and no others. They value themselves extremely for their Affinity to the English, and are ready to do them all friendly Offices. It is probable, that this Settlement miscarried for want of timely Supplies from England; or through the Treachery of the Natives, for we may reasonably suppose that the English were forced to cohabit with them, for Relief and Conversation; and that in process of Time, they conformed themselves to the Manners of their Indian relations."

History will never know for sure. White, of course, was anxious to push on for Hatteras and other possible native retreats. But the sailors were restless. Their food supplies were running low, and stormy seas made further quest a hazardous job. Besides, landing wasn't their idea in the first place.

This time the captain assented, and the ships sailed on to the West Indies for refitting and for rest. They returned to England in October, 1590.

That was the year Raleigh's patent was due to expire. Interest was fast waning. From time to time, English vessels made half-hearted attempts to locate the missing colonists. But none ever so much as penetrated the outer banks, and the visits were perfectly useless.

The English made subsequent attempts to establish colonies in the New World. But they concentrated then on the Chesapeake Bay area of Virginia, far to the north of Roanoke Island. The Carolina coast they gave back to the Indians.

Not until the latter part of the seventeenth century were those islands revisited. By then, all trace of the original colonists had been lost. And the mystery of their fate was indelibly impressed in the history of America's pioneers.

Engraving of Alexander I from *Russcaya Starina.—Photograph courtesy General Research and Humanities Division, The New York Public Library, Astor, Lenox and Tilden Foundations.*

THE
CASE
OF THE
EMPTY
COFFIN

---

*Czar
Alexander's
mysterious
"death" ...*

ROMANOV LEGENDS DIE hard.

In 1919, when the new Soviet government began relocating graves of the czars from the Cathedral of Saints Peter and Paul in Petrograd (formerly Saint Petersburg, now Leningrad), a favorite among these legends was reborn. For one of the graves, it was said, actually contained nothing more than an empty coffin.

According to this popular version of history, the Emperor Alexander I had only staged his death in 1825—and then gone on to live forty years more as a hermit in the cold woodlands of Siberia!

It was an old story, one painstakingly researched and later denied by the Grand Duke Nicholas Mikhailovitch, uncle of the last Romanov czar, Nicholas II. It was a puzzling story, full of intrigue and contradiction. And it has endured.

None of the mystery behind the legend has ever been confirmed or denied by any government of Russia.

It all began on the night of March 23, 1801, when Alexander's father, Paul I, still reigned. A force of sixty men, among them some of the country's leading noblemen and military officers, set out to raid the palace. For years they had secretly opposed Paul's regime, despised the emperor himself. Now they were determined to overthrow him. And they even had the tacit approval of Paul's eldest son and heir apparent, Alexander.

At eleven o'clock, they were admitted to the palace on a pretext. They went up a back staircase to the emperor's chambers. But a sentry stopped them at the door. They cut him down before he could so much as draw his sword.

The noise alarmed the emperor as he was preparing for bed. When he realized what had happened, he hid himself in his bedroom to pretend he'd escaped.

The ruse almost worked, too. But a Hanoverian general named Benningsen found him huddled behind a screen near the fireplace—barefoot and clad only in nightcap and gown.

"Sire," said the general, proclaiming the imminent change of command, "you are a prisoner by order of the Emperor Alexander."

At this point the conspirators were joined by a number of drunken stragglers who had got lost on their way to the coup. One of these newcomers slapped the emperor across the face. The emperor pushed him back. A struggle ensued. Paul was thrown to the floor, then kicked and strangled with an officer's scarf.

The murder cast a pall over the conscience of young Alexander. He was besieged by guilt feelings that grew stronger within him as the years went by. In the end they would consume him.

Meanwhile, at the age of twenty-three, he was his father's successor as Emperor and Autocrat of All the Russias. But he was a very different kind of "autocrat." Whereas Paul was cruel and authoritarian, Alexander was humane and progressive. Whereas Paul had made himself feared and hated, Alexander quickly won the people's love. He was hailed throughout the land and abroad as "Alexander the Blessed."

He surrounded himself with liberals, even formed a Committee on Public Welfare to guide him in planning large-scale reforms. The committee was the inner circle of his early government, his cabinet. It attacked such basic problems as the need for a constitution defining freedoms and responsibilities. It studied prospects for the abolition of serfdom.

Large sums of money were appropriated to establish a broad democratic educational system. Ministries were created to coordinate the government's administrative work justly and efficiently. The practice of torture was ended.

Ultimately, these plans fell short of completion. Failure was partly the fault of an unenlightened aristocracy bound by authoritarian tradition. The country was simply not ready for liberty.

More important, however, was a growing preoccupation with foreign affairs. For this was the era of Napoleon Bonaparte, the "Little Corporal." And all Europe was alive to the touch of his ambitions. His Grand Army was the terror of the continent. From Malta to Haiti he had cast the net of France's dreams of greater glory. Now he was at Russia's doorstep.

Eagerly, Alexander sought the means to peace with Napoleon. In July, 1807, the two men met on a raft on the Niemen River, near Prussia, to work out an agreement on their mutual aims. The result was the Treaty of Tilsit, a document regarded by Napoleon as a high point of his diplomatic career. Theoretically, at least, it formed a Franco-Russian alliance against Great Britain, the one European power constantly at war with the French conqueror. But the treaty also gave Alexander the time he needed to build a stronger defense against *any* European aggressor.

The treaty lasted only five years. In June, 1812, Napoleon led 600,000 men into Russia over that same Niemen River. By September, he had taken Moscow. But it was late in the season, nearly winter. And Napoleon's supplies were low. He had counted on a hard, quick victory, living off the land as he overran it. To make matters worse for him, the Muscovites set their city ablaze before retreating, and the French were left only ruins for a campsite. Finally, the Russian soldiers mounted forces to cut off Napoleon's escape by a southerly route.

Winter came earlier than usual and more severe. The invaders' vehicles and equipment bogged down in snow and ice. Men froze, starved, died. Of the surviving 200,000, half were taken prisoner.

It was the beginning of an inglorious end for the Grand Army of France.

Likewise, it was the peak of Alexander's own prestige. His country emerged one of the strongest in all Europe, he himself the most powerful sovereign on the continent.

Even as his power grew, however, he felt an increasing lack of confidence in himself. The haunting memories of his father's murder stained his glory. He felt a growing need to expiate himself of his sins, and he sought relief beyond the reach of human power.

In Switzerland, in 1813, he met a baroness, Madame von Krüdener, a diplomat's widow and mystic who had turned to religion after a professed life of sin. Her evangelistic entreaties made a deep impression on the troubled mind of the czar. Never particularly religious in his youth, Alexander now took to reading the Bible regularly. He held daily discourses with friends on the philosophic meanings of each passage he read. And he founded the Russian Bible Society to help spread the word among his people.

In Paris after the war, he presented his fellow monarchs with the covenant of a Holy Alliance—much as Woodrow Wilson would do a hundred years later with the League of Nations. It was a confederation based on the primacy of Christian law and the renunciation of war.

"Sublime mysticism and nonsense," Lord Castlereagh called it.

"High-sounding nothing," echoed the Austrian Prince Metternich.

Yet, they all signed the document as a mark of respect for the emperor's undoubted sincerity.

He had shown the sincerity of his belief in the reforms he sought during the early period of his reign. But he had had to let the quest slip out of his hands in order to cope with more pressing problems. And he had never been able to translate his ideals into a meaningful social program. The frustration of his efforts only made him the more aware of his failings as a man. He had been, as he put it, "crushed beneath the terrible burdens of a crown."

More than once he spoke of a desire to abdicate his title, to retire from official life altogether. As early as 1819, he had settled the matter of succession, naming as heir his brother Nicholas. At a dinner party that year, the czar told Nicholas and his wife, Alexandra, of his decision.

"More than ever," he said, "Europe needs young, strong monarchs. I am no longer the man I was. And I think it my duty to retire in time."

Over the years, a sense of guilt and ineffectiveness further sapped his strength. He became increasingly despondent, unconcerned with affairs of state. To add to his troubles, his wife, the Empress Elizabeth, fell gravely ill.

The year was 1825. Elizabeth's physicians called for complete rest. They even suggested a Mediterranean holiday for the royal couple, wintering in the temperate climate of the French Riviera or in Italy. But Alexander had another idea. He proposed Taganrog on the shore of the Sea of Azov. And the empress agreed.

Alexander's choice confounded even those closest to him. Taganrog was not exactly what the doctors ordered. It was a small frontier town, a fortress some one thousand miles from the capital at Saint Petersburg. The countryside was rough and swampy, the winters damp and windy and often quite cold.

The couple took the best house in town—a ten-room brick villa, modestly furnished, with a small backyard and a run-down orchard alongside it. They kept their staff to what they considered a bare minimum, including five military aides, three doctors, two ladies-in-waiting, and assorted household servants.

"It is necessary," Alexander said enigmatically, "that the transition to private life not be too abrupt."

They spent their days among the people, walking together through the streets of Taganrog, stopping in at some of the little shops, chatting leisurely with neighbors. Often they would drive along the shore.

Elizabeth rested. The love and companionship of her husband and the seclusion of their cottage proved ideal for her health. She was at ease and plainly happy.

"It is not difficult," she wrote to her mother in October, "to judge the good the Emperor does by his very presence in the region in which he finds himself. The effects of this are already felt."

But the melancholy that plagued Alexander did not pass. He was restive and distant. Late in October, he organized an expedition to review his forces in the Crimea, thus confirming the fears of some that he planned an invasion of the Ottoman Empire.

In fact, he went more for his own diversion than for any military purpose.

On the eve of his departure, he sat at a desk finishing some last-minute correspondence. It was a cloudy afternoon, growing dark. He rang for his valet to bring him candles. After awhile, however, the sky cleared, and there was no need for candlelight. The valet returned.

"I did not ring for you," Alexander said sharply. "Why do you disturb me?"

"Because candles burning in a room in daylight foretell death," the servant reminded him.

"You are right," the emperor agreed. "Take away the candles."

Next day, he set out on the journey that would eventually lead to his mysterious "death."

Alexander returned to Taganrog in mid-November. He was pale and lethargic. He suffered from chill. In the days that followed, he developed all the symptoms of a fever, complaining of nausea, headache, perspiration, and an insatiable thirst. His body temperature ran high. His own opinion was that he had a mild case of malaria. Others have since suggested typhus.

Diaries disclose that even his attendants could not agree on his condition, much less the cause of his illness. Where Prince Peter Volkonsky reports that the czar spent a good night on the seventeenth, the English doctor Sir James Wylie notes that he may have taken a turn for the worse. Where Wylie observes on the nineteenth that Alexander seems apathetic and feverish, the empress writes that he is feeling well and is in the best of spirits. Where the empress and Volkonsky agree that his condition on the twenty-first is unchanged from a relapse on the previous day, the doctor becomes suddenly optimistic about his patient's recovery.

Curiously, Elizabeth's diary ends with the events of November 23. One week later, at almost eleven o'clock in the morning of December 1, 1825, Alexander died.

"Our angel is in heaven," the czar's widow wrote his mother, the Empress Maria Fyodorovna.

Curiously, too, there was no priest on hand during the last days of his life—although one had come to him as recently as the twenty-seventh.

Almost at once questions arose; the mystery deepened.

Had the emperor really died? Or was he still alive and hidden somewhere among his people? Had he left Russia?

First, there was the matter of an autopsy. The doctors let a day and a half needlessly lapse before they undertook their examination. And when a report finally was issued, it seemed to refer to a body other than that of Alexander. Lesions of the brain were detected, indicating an advanced stage of syphilis. Yet, there had never been any evidence of syphilis in the emperor's medical history. And the spleen, which should have been enlarged in case of malaria, was found to be quite normal.

The official version attributed Alexander's death to "disease of the liver and other organs secreting bile." But the details are obscure and the verdict uncertain. One need only remember that, twenty-five years earlier, on the eve of Alexander's ascension to power, his murdered father's death had been attributed to apoplexy!

One doctor, in fact, stubbornly refused to agree to the report of Alexander's death. Although his name appeared on the emperor's death certificate, Dr. Dimitri Tarassov denied that he had ever signed it. The signature, he claimed, was a simple forgery.

The Empress Elizabeth herself gave rise to doubt over the "death" of Alexander. "Where can one find refuge from this life?" she wrote her own mother as early as November 23. "When one thinks one has arranged everything for the best and is able to enjoy it, a new and unexpected trial arises that upsets all one's plans and takes away the faculty of enjoying the fruit of so much effort."

She wrote the letter after she had spent the late afternoon and entire evening with her husband. Had she discerned the impossibility of his recovery? If so, why did she go to such pains to enter in her diary that the emperor was "distinctly better"? And why did she also attribute this opinion to Wylie when the doctor dutifully recorded a worsening condition?

Or had Alexander, instead, confided to her some secret plan to stage his death and subsequently disappear—alone?

Elizabeth's entry for the twenty-third was her last. Either she ceased to write these daily reports after her long talk with Alexander that evening or, later, portions of the diary were destroyed by the emperor's brother and successor, Nicholas I. Nicholas, after all, is known to have destroyed many other documents relating to the last days of Alexander.

Even the imperial succession bore earmarks of a planned death. For on that same date, November 23, Alexander notified his mother and his brother Constantine of his illness. Constantine, heir apparent by virtue of seniority, had agreed with Alexander six years earlier that their younger brother should be the one to assume the crown next.

"When the time to abdicate comes," Alexander had concluded, "I shall let you know, and you will then inform mother of your decision."

Now he conveyed the news indirectly to Constantine by an aide-de-camp, General Diebitch. But to the Empress Maria Fyodorovna he addressed a personal letter. That, too, disappeared soon after his death!

Adding fuel to the fires of disbelief, the aging mother refused to wait for Alexander's remains to be returned to Saint Petersburg. Instead, she set out hastily on a journey of her own to meet the funeral train en route and to identify her son's body for herself. Her later assurance that it was, indeed, the emperor's corpse seemed somehow less significant than her previous doubt.

For years Alexander had dreamed of the day he might withdraw from public life. Only a month earlier he had told Volkonsky of his wish to settle down soon along the Crimea and live out his life as a private citizen.

"I have served for twenty-five years," he remarked, "and even a simple soldier can retire after that much service."

Leonid Strakhovsky, one of the czar's most recent biographers, presents a fascinating theory of how that retirement was accomplished. Alexander, he relates, was joined on his Crimean tour by a military courier named Maskov. The courier was killed when the coach in which he was traveling missed a sharp bend in the road and overturned. Alexander seized upon this death as the opportunity for his escape.

Maskov was roughly the emperor's size. In time, natural decomposition would obscure his features. He might well be able to pass for the emperor himself. The body, therefore, accompanied the official party back to Taganrog in November.

This theory, of course, is more elaborate than most. None had previously named the substitute supplied by the emperor for a corpse at his own funeral. Some even went so far as to suggest that there was no corpse at all—that the coffin was empty, or weighted only by stones inside.

Rumor sprung up almost at once and lingered throughout the nineteenth century. One version had Alexander settling down to a simple hermit's life along the shores of the Gulf of Finland. Another had him roaming the wilds of Siberia, there to spend the remainder of his natural life atoning for his sins. Still another found him not in Siberia, not anywhere in Russia, but in Palestine as a pilgrim in search of salvation.

It was later whispered in the highest circles that the czar's nephew, Alexander II, had ordered the coffin opened for inspection and found it empty—and, afterward, that Alexander III had actually switched an empty coffin for the one with an impostor resting inside.

As recently as 1919, the rumors were still flying.

Not only was no action taken to quiet gossip at the time of the czar's supposed death, but the authorities themselves lent credence to popular suspicions. Despite tradition, the public was not permitted to view the body during its long journey back to the capital. And the funeral at Saint Petersburg was held in strictest secrecy, with only members of the imperial family present. That was just before midnight on March 13, 1826.

Ten years later, on September 16, 1836, the mystery was stirred anew. This time it began like a tale from a Russian storybook.

It was late afternoon. The sun shone brightly. A tall stranger came quietly riding on a white horse into the Siberian village of Krasnufimsk. He sought out a blacksmith there to shoe his mount. As he waited, he was approached by local policemen.

Who was he? they asked. And what was his business in their town? But the stranger would not answer, leaving them to assume the worst. He was arrested as a vagrant and sentenced to flogging and imprisonment.

While still in jail there, the stranger had one visitor. It was the Grand Duke Michael, Alexander's youngest brother. He had heard of the case as he was passing through and went straight to the authorities with threats of dire punishment for their actions.

After a long talk with the prisoner, however, the grand duke agreed not to prosecute. A short time later, he left town.

The stranger himself was deported, first to one place and then another. At Krasnorechensk, in 1842, he settled down to the life of a pious hermit, a monk, under the name of Fyodor Kuzmitch.

He took a small hut deep in the forest, where he spent his days at work and prayer. He was a vegetarian and often fasted as a sign of his religious conviction. He went regularly to the village church, but he refused, much to the horror of the local priest, to take communion. And he confounded the townspeople by his correspondence with and visits from various notables of Russian society—everyone from the Bishop of Irkutsk to the future Alexander II.

Mystery shrouded his arrival among the people of the village, mystery surrounded the asceticism of his life there. Over the years, many stories sprung up to account for his presence. And they all centered on his identity as the former emperor.

One told of a retired soldier who met him at the home of a local church official.

"It's our czar," he cried out, "our father, Alexander Pavlovitch!"

The hermit protested.

"I'm only a vagabond," he told the soldier. "If you go around telling people I'm a czar, you'll be sent to prison and I'll be forced to flee."

Yet, for all his protests, he was close enough to Russian nobility to act as patron to a young peasant girl whom he knew and admired. He had seen to her education himself, trained her in the ways of mysticism. In 1849, he sent her off on the first of two pilgrimages to the holy places of central Russia. He furnished her with letters of introduction to some of the country's most important people, including Count Dimitri Osten-Sacken, who at the hermit's bidding invited her to stay for several months as a guest of his estate.

It was there the girl first noticed the hermit's striking resemblance to the late Alexander I—even down to the way they both held their hands on their belts as they stood. For the Osten-Sackens had a large portrait of the former emperor hanging prominently in their main house.

When she later told Fyodor of her observations, tears welled in the old hermit's eyes. And he left the room to hide the greater emotion he felt.

In 1857, the girl left a second time. Two years later, still in central Russia, she married an army major and went off to live with him in Kiev until his death in 1864. When she then returned home to her former protector, she learned that he too had died.

All that remained, according to the biographer Strakhovsky, was a small pouch the old man had carried on a cord around his neck. Inside was a coded message from the Emperor Paul to his wife: "We have discovered a terrible flaw in our son. Count Pahlen informs me of Alexander's participation in the conspiracy. We must hide tonight, wherever it is possible."

If the hermit Fyodor Kuzmitch was, in reality, Alexander Pavlovitch, then he had borne his sin like a cross to the end of his life.

Police Authorities are Requested to Post this Circular for the Information of Police Officers and File a Copy of it for Future Reference.

MISSING SINCE AUGUST 6, 1930

HONORABLE JOSEPH FORCE CRATER,
JUSTICE OF THE SUPREME COURT, STATE OF NEW YORK

DESCRIPTION—Born in the United States—Age, 41 years; height, 6 feet; weight, 185 pounds; mixed grey hair, originally dark brown, thin at top, parted in middle "slicked" down; complexion, medium dark, considerably tanned; brown eyes; false teeth, upper and lower jaw, good physical and mental condition at time of disappearance. Tip of right index finger somewhat mutilated, due to having been recently crushed.

Wore brown sack coat and trousers, narrow green stripe, no vest; either a Panama or soft brown hat worn at rakish angle, size 6⅝, unusual size for his height and weight. Clothes made by Vroom. Affected colored shirts, size 14 collar, probably bow tie. Wore tortoise-shell glasses for reading. Yellow gold Masonic ring, somewhat worn; may be wearing a yellow gold, square-shaped wrist watch with leather strap.

COMMUNICATE with CHIEF INSPECTOR, POLICE DEPARTMENT, 18th Division, (Missing Persons Bureau), New York City. Telephone Spring 3100.

FILE NO. 13595

---

the
disappearance
of
Judge
Joseph Crater...

THE SHERIFF TOOK his men out along Sprain Road in Yonkers. The body, he'd been told, would probably lie no more than two and a half feet beneath the surface, at a spot near Jennifer Lane. He kept his men digging there for the better part of two days. When they were done, they had covered an area of about 5,000 square feet, churned up some 15,000 cubic feet of dirt, and found absolutely nothing.

It was another dead end in the 34-year, quarter-of-a-million-dollar search for the missing Joseph Force Crater, justice of the Supreme Court of New York State. In 1930, on the night of August 6, Crater shook hands with a dinner companion and said good-bye. Then he stepped into a cab on westbound Forty-fifth Street in New York City and rode straight into oblivion.

The political scandals that unfolded shortly thereafter, the sordid tales of patronage and payoffs, of frauds and frame-ups, combined to make this the most shocking and most talked-about disappearance of the twentieth century.

On the face of it, the promising career of Joe Crater was anything but scandalous. The son of an Easton, Pennsylvania fruit grocer, Crater was a highly respected lawyer, a graduate of Lafayette College and the Columbia University School of Law. He was conservative in his manner, even a bit old-fashioned. His idea of courting his wife-to-be, Stella Wheeler, was to sit around the parlor with her family in the evening. Sometimes he would play the piano for them, and they would all sing along—popular songs of the day, like "Cuddle Up a Little Closer" and "They Wouldn't Believe Me." He himself sang softly, tenderly, as he played the strains of his old fraternity anthem, "The Sweetheart of Sigma Chi."

Joe Crater was a club man to the end.

Physically, he stood six feet tall, erect and broad-shouldered. He had a long and skinny neck that he tried to hide with a high, starched collar. In all, he looked more like a stern small-city banker than the big-city playboy he was known by some to be.

His wardrobe was large and impressive—the suits custom-made by Vroom, one of New York's most exclusive tailors. He insisted that Stella follow his lead by patronizing only the better women's shops.

He had a fondness for the theater—Broadway musicals, comedies, serious dramas, even out-of-town tryouts. He loved first nights and was always willing to pay agency prices for two seats front and center. For him it always had to be front and center.

In his legal career, too, he aimed as high as he could see. He made no secret of his ambition someday to gain a seat on the United States Supreme Court. And there were many who thought he'd make it.

For Crater was more than a man of dreams, more than a man of drive. He had a talent and a love for the law that were not easily matched. Compiling a superior record at Columbia Law, he had gone on to teach at Fordham, and later was appointed assistant professor at New York University. Wherever he lectured, he was recognized as one of the most entertaining and most instructive men that ever graced a podium.

But success wasn't quick enough that way.

"I would rather teach law," he told his wife, "but above that there are many things I would like you to have out of life and mere teaching certainly will not provide them. So I have decided that the best way to get ahead is to go into politics."

The famed Seabury investigations would soon disclose just how profitable those politics could be. Under the auspices of an efficient and powerful Tammany machine, city building and housing codes had become a moneyed farce; criminal rackets were commonplace, police bribery rampant. Contempt for the public was institutionalized in a favorite clubhouse ballad:

The suckers will vote in the fall, tra la,
The suckers will vote in the fall.

Even the judgeships were up for grabs—one year's pay for a seat on the bench. As early as July, 1930, the bribery of party leaders for appointments had come into the open with an investigation into the affairs of George F. Ewald. Ewald, a Traffic Court magistrate, was charged with having paid Tammany leader Martin J. Healy $10,000 for the position.

And who was the chief speaker at Ewald's celebration dinner on the eve of his appointment to the court? None other than the president of Healy's own Cayuga Democratic Club in the nineteenth assembly district of Manhattan, Joseph Force Crater!

By then, Crater was already on the edge of the big time in state and local politics. He was on easy terms with men like former Governor Alfred E. Smith and the renowned Senator Robert F. Wagner. In 1920, in fact, when Wagner himself was a judge on the State Supreme Court, he employed Crater as his confidential secretary—acknowledging him as "one of the best new minds in the New York legal field."

When Wagner prepared to move to Washington, Crater set up his own law practice. But the senator kept him close by, leasing him office space in his own New York City quarters. And when another Supreme Court justice, Joseph M. Proskauer, retired in April, 1930, Wagner suggested to Governor Franklin D. Roosevelt that he nominate his protégé to fill the unexpired term.

The nomination was crucial. It implied election to a full fourteen-year term in November. Roosevelt was caught in the crossfire of an Al Smith-Tammany Hall battle for the right to name Proskauer's successor. He turned to Wagner for advice and came up with Crater as the perfect compromise candidate. The *New York Times* lauded the choice as non-political and declared the nominee "well qualified to be on the bench of the Supreme Court."

Clearly, Joe Crater was a man on his way to the top.

Then, on the evening of August 2, while vacationing with his wife at their summer cottage in Maine, he got a mysterious telephone call. Who called the judge or what was said between them was never learned. But it was enough to send him packing.

"I've got to straighten those fellows out," he told Stella cryptically.

Next morning, he boarded the Bar Harbor Express for New York. She never saw him again.

In New York, Crater went first to his Fifth Avenue apartment. He told the maid he'd only be in town a few days. He had to leave, he said, in time to be back with his wife on her birthday, the ninth. Then he suggested that she herself take a few days off.

That afternoon, August 4, Crater briefly visited his chambers in the courthouse downtown and paid a visit to his physician in Greenwich Village. The doctor, Augustus Rizzi, a personal friend, invited the judge to dinner at his house the next night.

The judge spent the next day, the fifth, tending to a backlog of legal business, pausing at noon for lunch with two fellow justices. That night, he kept his dinner date with the Rizzis, staying on until well past midnight. First thing in the morning, he was back in his chambers.

That was August 6. His only visitor was Simon Rifkind, the man who had succeeded him as Wagner's secretary. When Rifkind was gone, Crater called in his assistant, Joe Mara. Hurriedly, he wrote and endorsed two checks totaling $5,100 and sent him off to cash them at once. "Get large bills," he demanded.

By the time the young man returned with the money, Crater had bundled up papers from his office files into four large portfolios and two briefcases. He asked Mara to help him take them home. Mara did, and probably the judge spent that entire afternoon working on those files in his apartment. No trace was ever found of them, either.

"According to Mara," Police Commissioner Mulrooney told reporters, "the judge told him he was going up Westchester way and pledged Mara to say nothing in his absence."

By seven, Crater had finished his work and decided to spend the evening uptown, along Broadway, perhaps taking in the Belasco's recent hit comedy, *Dancing Partners*. A ticket agent he knew told him there was no single ticket immediately available. But he was sure he could get one for the judge before show time. He would leave it at the box office in the judge's name.

Crater still had time for dinner. He walked along West Forty-fifth Street to the Billy Haas Restaurant, between Eighth and Ninth avenues, on the site of what is now the east wing of a large, drab apartment building. There he met a friend, a Shubert Brothers lawyer named Klein, and the friend's friend, a Shubert Brothers chorus girl named Ritz. They invited Crater to join them.

The three ate leisurely, not leaving the restaurant until 9:15. Curtain time was 8:40. But this did not deter Crater. He was still eager to see the play, he said, even if he had already missed most of the first act.

He paid his check and went outside with the others. He shook hands with Klein, hailed a taxi, and got inside. Then, he waved good-bye.

It was the last anyone ever saw of him.

Stella, meanwhile, was biding her time at their summer place 400 miles away. Her birthday, the ninth, came and went. Still there was no sign of her husband, no word from him either. There was only the quiet, anxious waiting. Finally, on the fifteenth, she sent their family chauffeur, Fred Kahler, to New York to find out where the judge was and when he was coming back.

Kahler drove down alone. He went first to the apartment, where the maid told him that Crater hadn't been around since she returned on the eighth. Next he phoned some of the judge's friends, who quickly sought to reassure him. They warned the chauffeur against making much of a stir just before the November elections.

They, too, were undoubtedly bothered by the disappearance. But they had to reckon also with the possibility that Crater was off on some kind of spree that might not sparkle in the glare of wide publicity. The judge, they knew, was quite the ladies' man. In fact, he had just returned from a showgirl-accompanied jaunt to Atlantic City when he left for Maine on August 1.

Kahler thus returned to Maine with high hopes. Patiently, he and Stella waited for the twenty-fifth, the opening date of the court's Special Term. Crater's political friends had all but promised that the judge would put in his appearance then. But they were wrong. Crater never made it.

Now Stella hurried home to New York, where a city detective and Wagner bodyguard, Leo Lowenthal, had already begun an unofficial search for the missing judge.

"Senator Wagner is on his way back from Europe," Lowenthal told the distraught woman. "I don't think anything should be done until he gets here."

But the New York *World* did not agree. On September 3, the paper broke its story of the disappearance on page one. Next day, Rifkind went through the formality of asking the police department's Bureau of Missing Persons to look into the case.

This was exactly four weeks and a day after the judge had vanished!

The time lag alone seriously hindered the hunt. Clues had already been lost. Memories of witnesses had begun to fade. Any trace there might have been of Crater had long since been covered over, inadvertently or not.

Another impediment was Crater's wife. At least, Manhattan District Attorney Thomas Crain saw it that way. He had questions he wanted to ask Stella, a lot of questions. But she left again for her Maine hideaway before the news was out and was not about to return to New York with a spotlight focused on her, to be interrogated like a common witness in a police case.

However, she did make one concession. She permitted Crain to file some thirty questions with her for written replies. This he did, grudgingly. But even on paper the answers were not all an anxious DA might have hoped. Obviously, Mrs. Crater was not privy to details of the judge's financial or private affairs. Obviously, too, she was not in the mood to elaborate on those questions she might be able or willing to answer.

The investigation proved fruitless. A grand jury heard nearly a thousand pages of courtroom testimony (including Mrs. Crater's answers to further written questioning by the court). It scanned over 600 letters, depositions, and other communications sent from all parts of the country and abroad. Yet, on November 7, it had to conclude that it could not reach any valid, positive decision concerning the fate or whereabouts of Joseph F. Crater.

"His effacement," one newspaper reported, "has been so complete as to be incredible."

Overnight the name became synonymous with the act of disappearing. When anyone dropped out of sight for a while, newspaper columnists accused him of "pulling a Crater." Night club and vaudeville comics used the name as a running gag ("Look, there goes Judge Crater!").

Not everyone was laughing, though. To many it seemed an obvious case of murder—the more so as the years wore on.

One favorite set of theories among amateur detectives has centered on the judge's acquaintance with other women. Stella's lawyer, Emil K. Ellis, developed a variation on this theme into a full-blown courtroom case. Crater, he said, had been lured into an ex-girl friend's flat for a blackmail payoff, but reacted angrily when she upped the ante on him.

He was "encouraged" by her companions to simmer down. But he was "encouraged" just a little too hard.

Maybe it was unintentional, Ellis conceded, but it was still murder. The body may have been subsequently cremated or even stuffed inside an empty bronze statue and dropped into the river gangland style. Names of local underworld enforcers were mentioned, names like Harry Stein and "Chowderhead" Cohen.

Yet, what about all those papers, the ones the judge had taken home on the morning of that last day? What was their connection with the disappearance? And where had they gone?

Most likely, the papers bore on the various intrigues of Crater's career. They might have included the coincidental withdrawal of $23,000 from his stock and bank accounts—shortly after his appointment to that $22,500-a-year court post in April. Or they may even have had something to do with his handling of the Libby Hotel receivership the previous year.

The hotel was a bankrupt corporation comprising many small investors. It had been sold by Crater, in his capacity as receiver, to a finance company for $75,000 in June, 1929. Six weeks later, it was resold to the city, which wanted the site for a street widening project. Resale price: $2,800,000.

Somebody made a lot of money that summer. There were those who felt that Crater got a handsome piece of it.

Narrating the circumstances of her husband's disappearance, Stella Crater has recalled an interesting episode. It took place in July, 1929, when she and Joe made a spur-of-the-moment motor trip into Canada. Just as they were starting back from Quebec, the judge suddenly told Kahler to pull over alongside a bank near the edge of town. He wanted to exchange some currency, he said.

"Much later," Stella relates in her autobiography, "as events developed, I often wondered if it was possible that he had gone in there to make a deposit. It has been one of those idle questions which frequently has intrigued and puzzled me over the years."

What if there were, indeed, a deal brewing to divvy up the Libby Hotel profits? What better reason for a killing among thieves than to increase the shares of the dead man's surviving partners?

Or, perhaps, as has been repeatedly suggested, Crater promised a year's pay for his judgeship, then reneged after the appointment. Maybe he was overcome with pangs of integrity, maybe he was just plain scared of another Healy-Ewald scandal. That, too, would be a classic motive.

Another possibility suggests itself at the mention of Crater's mysterious phone call—the one he got in Maine that sent him scurrying for the files in his New York office to "straighten those fellows out." Could the caller have told him that it was the party leaders themselves who feared another scandal? Could he have learned, then, that the deal was off, that he would not be nominated for election to a full term in November?

Maybe, say some of the murder theorists, he went to New York to remind his cronies of a few hard facts, such as his knowledge of certain shady deals and practices that had been so common in years past. What's more, he had the documents to prove it. These he carefully sifted from his office files and hid away. Then he kept his date with "those fellows" in Westchester County—only to be forever silenced.

One neglected fact of the investigations, however, was a passing reference to Crater's heart condition. Joseph Grainsky, the Broadway ticket agent who got Crater a seat for *Dancing Partners,* was also a good friend of the judge. As a matter of fact, he and Crater had gone swimming together on that trip the judge made to Atlantic City earlier in the summer. Crater, though, had soon come out of the water. As Grainsky told the grand jury, the judge was complaining of pains in his chest.

Interestingly, Mrs. Crater, when asked during the later probe for the name of her husband's physician, said he was Dr. Hugh M. Cox. Yet, one of Crater's first visits in New York that fateful week was to his doctor friend, Augustus Rizzi.

"I don't know of his relations to Dr. Rizzi," Simon Rifkind recently told this author. "Judge Crater was not in the habit of complaining about physical ailments. I have never known him to complain of a bad heart."

Perhaps, then, Crater wanted to check out his suspicions quietly, without exciting his wife or political associates. Perhaps those suspicions were well founded, and sometime on the seventh or eighth of August he suffered a fatal heart attack in the heat of argument with "those fellows"—or even out swimming. In a panic to keep the charge of murder from Tammany's doorstep, Crater's companions hastily buried the body nearby and let the judge just "disappear."

The mystery was compounded the following January with the discovery of four manila envelopes in the judge's bureau drawer. No such envelopes had been seen during any of four police searches of the Crater apartment. None had been seen when the detective Lowenthal searched earlier. None had been seen by any of the grand jurors who searched later. But there they were nonetheless: four envelopes containing some $6,690 in cash, insurance policies on the judge's life for $30,000, a note in Crater's hand itemizing the money due him on several small loans (including reference to "Libby Hotel—there will be a very large sum due me for services when the city pays the 2¾ million in condemnation"), and a brief will leaving everything to Stella.

It was Stella who found the envelopes.

Had they really been there all the while? If not, who put them there? Crater's murderers, stricken with remorse for the widow's plight? A friend of Crater's, acting on the judge's instructions? Perhaps Crater himself? Or were they in

Stella's possession from the beginning, brought down by her from Maine to be "discovered" in a more suitable place?

"I think someone," District Attorney Crain answered a reporter for the *Herald Tribune*, "had access to the apartment and put the money and papers in the drawer between the time the apartment was searched and the arrival of Mrs. Crater. . . . Mrs. Crater, when she told us of her discovery, had all the appearance of a heart-broken woman telling the truth."

No matter. The trail of Joe Crater was already growing cold.

Over the next four decades he would be "sighted" by one person after another in just about every part of the world. He was a recluse in Nova Scotia, a bingo operator in Africa, a corpse in the Hungarian cemetery at Perth Amboy, New Jersey. But none of these discoveries would ever pan out.

In 1955, Murray Teigh Bloom, an American writer, presented a photograph of Crater to a Dutch clairvoyant named Gerard Croiset. The seer studied the back of the picture, rubbed his finger along the surface, and went into a trance. Before he came out, he had drawn a pencil sketch outlining New York City's five boroughs. He made an "X" in mid-Manhattan, where the man in the picture had disappeared. Then, he made another "X" just above the northern edge of the Bronx, in Westchester County. There, he said, on the first floor of a Dutch farmhouse, the judge was killed; and there outside the house he was buried.

At a later sitting, he pinpointed the exact site of Crater's grave.

Strangely enough, the details checked out with Missing Persons in New York. Until then, the existence of the house had been a guarded secret—only recently learned by the police themselves from a dying East Harlem butcher named Henry Krauss. It was his house Croiset had "X"ed. Krauss had been a Cayuga Club regular in the twenties and early thirties. Since he used his Westchester place only on weekends, he made it freely available at all other times to his political cronies—including Crater and Healy. One Sunday, Krauss said, he had driven up to the house and found the kitchen littered with liquor and beer bottles and covered with blood.

That was August 10, 1930. The coincidence of Crater's disappearance later convinced him that the judge had been murdered there. But he could not explain why the killers would have left such a mess to tell the tale.

In 1959, an excavation was made near the house. But it turned up nothing.

Again, in 1964, Westchester authorities went digging on the basis of further information from Croiset. This time the grounds they plowed were opposite a country club, and three elements of the seer's story fit perfectly: a cluster of trees, an abandoned road, and a pond that had long since been covered over. They found everything, it seems, but the body.

As the sheriff in charge sadly noted: "There wasn't even a bone some dog might have buried for future reference."

And so the case of the lost judge—to New York City cops it's Missing Persons File No. 13595—is as open today as it ever was.

＊　　＊

A curious parallel to the disappearance of Joseph Crater is to be found in the annals of New York City history. One hundred years earlier, on December 12, 1829, John Lansing walked out of a prominent downtown hotel and was never seen or heard from again.

Lansing was, wrote a nineteenth-century historian, "one of the most distinguished Americans of his time." Like Crater, he had been a justice of the State Supreme Court. He was a large man, too, dignified and convivial. Recognized for his superior legal mind, Lansing quickly became a protégé of the Clinton family, as powerful a political machine as New

York ever had. His career was a sure success.

He served in the State Assembly for six terms, was elected to Congress under the Articles of Confederation, and went with Alexander Hamilton and Robert Yates as a New York delegate to the Constitutional Convention in 1787. For four years he was mayor of Albany.

In 1790, Lansing was named to the Court, succeeding Yates as chief justice in 1798. Three years later, he was made chancellor of New York State, a top governing post, which he filled until he reached the statutory retirement age of sixty in 1814.

He returned to legal practice after that and served as regent of the University of the State of New York. He also acted in an unofficial capacity on behalf of Columbia College, and it was on such business that he traveled to New York City in December, 1829.

On the twelfth of the month, he left the rotunda of his hotel, near the site where Joe Crater would later hang out his shingle at 120 Broadway. The last person to see him was the hallboy who dusted off his coat. Lansing told him he was going to mail a letter on the Albany boat at the foot of Cortlandt Street.

In the gray light of early evening, he vanished. A close investigation followed. But it never turned up the slightest clue.

Years later, the famed editor-lobbyist Thurlow Weed claimed he had been told the inside story of Lansing's death. It was, he said, a plain case of murder. The ex-judge knew too much about a certain case involving the interests of some politically influential people.

"Descendants of Lansing who investigated his story," writes Joseph Strayer, the judge's biographer, "were satisfied that it had no basis in fact."

Others at the time recalled the bitter fight that had erupted when Lansing, as chancellor, sentenced a distinguished

Albany lawyer to prison. The lawyer later sued for unlawful imprisonment but lost the case.

All that, however, was a score of years earlier—and a very long time to wait to settle a grudge.

Strayer feels the likelihood greater that Lansing simply lost his footing on the pier, stumbled into the river, and was swept out to sea. Either that, he says, or else he was mugged —yes, even in those days!—on his way to the boat.

In any case, they never found that body either.

FROM
MU
TO
GONDWANALAND

---

*the
mysterious
worlds
of
prehistoric man . . .*

IN THE BEGINNING there was Mu. That, anyway, is the story told by James Churchward, the most popular and most prolific historian of this fabulous "lost" continent.

According to Churchward, Mu dated all the way back to about 20,000 B.C. The continent was located in the mid-Pacific, a huge mass of flat terrain straddling the equator. It was covered with tropical vegetation. And it was inhabited by no less than 64 million people.

These people were divided into ten tribes, with all races represented among them but with whites naturally supreme. The entire population was governed by a high priest called Ra, whose monotheistic religion was later emulated by the prophet Jesus Christ.

The continent of Mu lasted, Churchward says, nearly 19,000 years—a span more than three times as great as our own recorded history. Both culturally and technologically, its people developed to an incredibly high level of sophistication. Yet, when the end finally came, their civilization almost entirely disappeared. Remnants of it served as the basis of subsequent cultures.

The end came, it seems, sometime during the twelfth century B.C., when "gas belts" at the earth's core collapsed. The result was a succession of upheavals that sank the continent into the great sea.

As a storyteller, Churchward is probably unsurpassed. But he suffers several shortcomings as a scholar. Many of these have been pointed out by Lyon Sprague de Camp in his comprehensive study, *Lost Continents*.

The whole history of Mu, as Churchward tells it, is derived from just two sets of tablets. One of them, strangely enough, was never seen by anyone but himself. It had been secretly shown to him by an aged priest in India when he was stationed there as a colonel in the British army. The other has long been known to archeologists as nothing more than a work of ancient art. In each case, quite by chance, Churchward discovered the "key" to translation just before he came upon the document itself.

Churchward, says de Camp, is guilty of serious misquotations in establishing his case. Furthermore, he "printed various nonsensical footnotes reading '4. Greek record.' or '6. Various records.' When he printed a table of forty-two Egyptian hieroglyphs, only six of them were even remotely correct."

Somewhat more credible is the history of Lemuria. The name itself is derived from the lemur, a mammal related to the monkey with a foxlike face and the nocturnal habits of an owl. The animal is found today chiefly in the Malagasy Republic, an island off the east coast of Africa. However, specimens exist on the continent as well as in the Orient, largely in India. This fact led nineteenth-century biologists and paleontologists to speculate that there had once been a large land bridge linking the two continents of Africa and Asia.

Such a possibility had been previously suggested by similarities of rock and fossil formations in South Africa and in the central regions of India. Geologists have dated these deposits from the Permian period, toward the end of the Paleozoic era. This would go back not only further than the age of man and mammals; it would also precede the age when dinosaurs and giant lizards ruled the earth.

A number of Darwinian biologists have thus contended that this "lost" continent was the original home of man. Here the mammal came to life. Here the process of man's evolution began. This, they say, accounts for the prevalence of lemurs on the isle of Malagasy to this day.

Lemuria, legendary land of the lemur, would seem, therefore, to be a geographical "missing link," representing what was once a united Afro-Asian continent.

Some investigators have carried this logic one step further. The "link," they say, was part of what was in fact a supercontinent, one that very nearly circled the globe. It stretched across the southern hemisphere and included Africa and the nearby Malagasy Republic, India, Australia and the island state of Tasmania, South America and the Falkland Islands off the coast of Argentina, and the Antarctic. (Interestingly, the one gap in this huge land mass existed just where Churchward insisted on locating his "lost" continent of Mu—right in the middle of the Pacific Ocean!)

This supercontinent is called Gondwanaland (or Gondwana-Land), a name conferred on it by the celebrated Austrian geologist Eduard Suess "after the ancient Gondwána flora which is common to all its parts." It is said to have existed long before Lemuria. In fact, many theorists claim that, if Lemuria ever did exist, it did so only as a remnant of that supercontinent; it was simply the last of several portions to sink into the sea.

Indeed, the German meteorologist Alfred Wegener proposed in the 1920s that Gondwanaland itself had been but half of an earlier supercontinent, Pangaea, dating back some 200 million years. But it is only recently that his notions of continental breakup and drift have been accorded the serious attention of the scientific community.

"Wegener," said a *New York Times* editorial in late 1969, "it now appears likely, did for geology what Copernicus did for astronomy, providing a pattern that brings order and understanding to a vast collection of seemingly unrelated facts."

Gondwanaland thus becomes the cloth of which the modern world is cut. On the basis of Suess' studies, de Camp has reconstructed the sequence of the supercontinent's breakup:

> Australia and New Zealand separated first, which fact accounts for their lack of placental mammals, since placental mammals had not been invented at the time of the separation. South America went next. . . .
> The last part to sink was the land-bridge connecting South Africa with India, the geologists' Lemuria, leaving

Madagascar [now the Malagasy Republic] and the great Seychelles Reefs with their islands as a fossil of its former existence. . . .

Some geologists, notably American, have taken exception to the theory. At most, they claimed, there were narrow land bridges connecting the several continents we know today; but there was no one giant comprising them all.

Nevertheless, the theory of a supercontinent accounts for many phenomena not otherwise easily explained. These include the striking similarities among flora and fauna in altogether disparate regions of the earth. The theory is also compatible with certain fundamental geologic processes.

Most accounts of "lost" continents date from periods of earthly turmoil, of earthquakes and floods. Not only were whole land masses sunk, but remaining terrain was completely rearranged. Solid earth was in many areas compressed and forced into mountainous shapes of varying size. This process is what geologists call "orogeny." And it is by such activity that, in the course of hundreds of millions of years, the planet has presumably taken its present form out of what was originally a flat land surface.

It is by such activity, too, that we may conveniently, though doubtfully, tie together all the tales of lands that might have been: Pangaea, Gondwanaland, Lemuria, possibly even the fabulous Mu. Orogeny may have accounted for the earthly spasms that led finally to the loss of that most celebrated of all lost continents: the island empire of Atlantis.

TOWERS
OF TOPAZ,
TREES
OF PEARL

---

*the
lost
continent
of
Atlantis . . .*

PERHAPS IT'S ONLY part of a fairy tale, the fable of a land that never was. Perhaps it once was something more. For this was Atlantis, and there are those who say the civilization it spawned may have inspired our own.

Its story goes back beyond the recorded history of man. In fact, according to the Greek philosopher Plato, the story goes back to about the year 10,000 B.C.

He tells of the nation's rise, its greatness in an era we now know only as primitive and barbaric. And he tells of its literal fall—its submergence in the ocean it had dominated:

> But afterwards there occurred violent earthquakes and floods, and in a single day and night of misfortune all your warlike men in a body sank into the earth, and the island of Atlantis in like manner disappeared in the depths of the sea. For which reason the sea in those parts is impassable and impenetrable, because there is a shoal of mud in the way; and this was caused by the subsidence of the island.

By word of mouth the tale was handed down. Improved upon, embellished, enriched with heroes and with gods, it made its way into the lore of Arabian geographers and afterward was set down as undisputed fact by medieval writers.

Subsequently, however, the ages of reason and enlightenment prevailed. Empiricists raised their doubts. And by the eighteenth century, the truth of the Atlantis epic had been debated by such illustrious personages as Voltaire, Montaigne, and Buffon.

The years since then have not been kind to legend. Yet, for all the latter-day skepticism and outright scoffing, the possibility of a continent virtually lost at sea remains; and the story of Atlantis has never relinquished its charm and its perplexity.

Thus the twentieth-century poet Conrad Aiken began his own account:

There was an island in the sea
That out of immortal chaos reared
Towers of topaz, trees of pearl,
For maidens adored and warriors feared.

Since then, that "island in the sea" has been the subject
of a thousand books and articles. It has become a symbol of
utopia, the fantasy of a world apart. It has been romanticized,
idealized, but never lost.

Now, in this age of scientific discovery and fantastic voyages into space, we find evidence that the old story of
Atlantis may not have been a myth. The island kingdom, it
seems, may really have existed, once dominating the region
that now comprises parts of Southern Europe, Asia, and
Africa.

Recent archeological expeditions have uncovered the remains of an ancient Minoan community at Thera, an Aegean
island off the coast of Greece. Radioactive carbon dating of
ash samples located there has fixed the time of its existence
as contemporary with the supposed era of Atlantis—some ten
centuries before the birth of Christ. And a number of the
world's leading scientists are thus convinced not only that
there was an Atlantean civilization long before Plato's day
but that Thera was actually a part of it.

What kind of a land was it, then, this prehistoric Atlantis?
Who were its people? And why was it destroyed? The questions of modern science turn us back again to the lessons of
the ancient philosopher.

In the two dialogues *Timaeus* and *Critias* Plato locates the
empire "in front of the straits which are by you called the
pillars of Heracles [the Strait of Gibraltar]." The entire area,
which he describes as larger than all of Libya and Asia
combined, is roughly the same as that we know now as the
Middle East.

Descended from the sea god Poseidon, the Atlanteans were
extraordinarily powerful, brave, handsome, dextrous people.

They wrought a civilization the likes of which had never before been achieved. And they soon extended their power to far-distant lands.

As they grew in earthly size and possessions, however, these Atlanteans became further removed from the godhead of their birth. They became increasingly mortal in their weaknesses and their corruption. In the end they met their match in the warriors of Athens.

That first great loss foretold somehow their ultimate doom. Soon afterward came the great explosions and the tidal waves that sank the mighty sons of Poseidon to the bottom of the sea.

For centuries, the most distinguished scholars of antiquity have pondered the lesson of these dialogues. Indeed, many of them have said the story was meant to be nothing more than that—a lesson for scholars, a mythical case study.

"Plato," concluded the late Edith Hamilton, one of the most learned and articulate of them all, "is again resting his mind. He is making up a fairy tale, the most wonderful island that could be imagined."

For Atlantis, to Plato, was in many ways the ideal commonwealth. Many years earlier, he had written his classic *Republic* to describe the form of government and social structure best suited to the principle of justice. The state, he emphasized, was in the final analysis no more than an extension of the individual citizen. Here in these later, somewhat lesser, works, *Timaeus* and *Critias,* he seized upon a "historical" entity to carry his case a step further—to the confederation of states as an extension of local government. The story thus becomes a kind of science-fiction postscript to his masterpiece.

Recent excavations at Thera, however, leave room for doubt—or, rather, for a certain measure of belief in the philosopher's tale. Implying as they do the destruction of the site by volcanic eruption, these archeological findings are wholly consistent with Plato's account of the island's geography. And Plato took pains to describe that geography fully.

Basically, the central city of Atlantis was laid out on a hill in a circular pattern of alternating canals and land strips—something on the order of modern Amsterdam. A huge waterway traversed all these rings from the ocean to the temple of Poseidon at the city's core, which was at the very peak of the hill.

Aspects of Plato's general description have convinced some archeologists that the seat of that Atlantean empire rested on a partially submerged volcano. Such a notion is enhanced by Plato's specific references to springs of both hot and cold water there on the island. Furthermore, a recent parallel points out the physical possibilities of volcanic destruction.

In 1883, tremendous eruptions very nearly obliterated Krakatoa, an island volcano west of Java in the Indian Ocean, near Sumatra. Whole villages were wiped out by the tremors and the gigantic waves that followed. In all, some 40,000 people were killed.

The island itself had long been considered to have been merely the remnant of a larger, prehistoric piece of land, perhaps also an island. It is said to have been splintered by a series of volcanic shocks into several small islands, all of which were eventually submerged. The last to go was the central peak of the volcano, Krakatoa, which was blown to bits less than a century ago.

There is no proof, of course, that Atlantis was an island volcano—or even that it was located on the site of modern Thera. But many of the participants in recent diggings there believe firmly in the identity. Among them is James W. Mavor, Jr., a naval architect and engineer with the Woods Hole (Massachusetts) Oceanographic Institution.

It was Mavor who, in 1966, began this speculation with an expedition he had organized to take seismic and magnetic profiles of the ocean bottom and subbottom of the sea around Thera. His findings, released the following year, indicated the distinct possibility that volcanic eruption had accounted for the earthquake and flooding that overwhelmed the region.

Whether out of professional jealousy or an increased nationalistic spirit, Mavor has been barred from further exploration in the area by a military junta that seized control of the Greek government in 1967. (Mavor himself, in correspondence with the author, asserts unequivocally that the action against him was one of "primarily jealousy.")

Despite this barrier to further investigation, Mavor clings to his earlier contention. "I believe that our work on Thera," he writes in his recently published *Voyage to Atlantis*, "has substantiated [Plato's account] as credible history. . . . The solution of the mystery of Atlantis should also, in my view, encourage the wider application of physical science to understanding these prehistoric memories, so as to re-create the topography, the weather, the climate, the ocean currents, the shorelines, the soil, the complete environmental situation out of which the myths sprang."

It is, of course, still possible that the Edith Hamiltons are right. Perhaps the philosopher Plato never meant his story of Atlantis as anything more than a fairy tale, a fable of magnificence on which to build his classic studies of government and justice.

But, then again, an increasing body of scientific research does point to the existence of (*a*) a great land mass in that area he described as "in front of the straits . . . called the pillars of Heracles" and (*b*) some global catastrophe that shook and inundated the region, wiping out whatever civilization might have developed there. Possibly Plato seized upon these truths, projected them into a history of his own device, and drew his own moral conclusions.

And, if there be some bit of truth to the tale, then various exciting possibilities at once arise: Whatever happened to the natives of Atlantis? Were they utterly destroyed in that doomsday chaos? If not, what has become of the survivors? How did they escape? Where did they go?

All that, of course, is quite another story.

WHO DISCOVERED AMERICA?

---

ancient
civilizations
of
the
"New World" ...

THE STORY OF America begins with Columbus. At least, that's the way most history books tell it. Some start as far back as the voyages of Leif Ericsson, 500 years earlier, then hurry on to Columbus' discovery of the New World and the subsequent infusion into it of European culture.

But there are cultural similarities between Europe and America in evidence long before the advent of Columbus—or even Ericsson and his Viking crew.

Ignatius Donnelly, a Minnesota politician-turned-historian of the late 1800s, summarized many of these in a classic study. The ancient Mayas, he said, shared with the peoples of Europe and Asia a belief in the immortality of the soul; worship of the sun, moon, and planets; an agrarian economy; and a caste system that involved, among other things, inheritance by the son of his father's trade. It seemed incredible to Donnelly that these and many other common traits could have come about by sheer coincidence.

A contemporary of Donnelly's, the archeologist James Ferguson, noted striking resemblances between the architectural style of Mediterranean builders and that of ancient Peru:

> The sloping jambs, the window cornice, the polygonal masonry, and other forms so closely resemble what is found in the old Pelasgic cities of Greece and Italy, that it is difficult to resist the conclusion that there may be some relation between them.

At Tiahuanaco, the famed "lost city" in the heartland of Inca civilization, there stand huge monuments of wholly mysterious origin. They are constructed in a style unlike anything ever done by the Incas themselves; indeed, they most likely antedate that comparatively modern Indian tribe by several centuries.

In language, too, one finds strong likenesses. Even the name of the Indian god Hurakan readily suggests the

European vocabulary of deluge and destruction: the English *hurricane,* the Spanish *huracán,* the French *ouragan,* the Italian *uragano,* the German *Orkan.* According to legend, it was this god Hurakan who brought on the catastrophic flood attributed to others in Babylonian and biblical literature.

Such similarities are not only fascinating but historically inconceivable. For, despite the common aspects of their folkways, architecture, and language, *there has never been any known link between the two civilizations.* It is widely accepted today that the Indians of North America were descended from Asiatic stock moving eastward and across Alaska. But the tribes of South America have never been accounted for.

Whence did these people come? Were they descendants of some other ancient people—say, Mediterranean—who, unknown to history, migrated to South America and reestablished on her shores the civilization of their former land? Or had they, in fact, originated in South America and, again unknown to history, developed a civilization of their own so closely parallel to those of Europe and Asia?

For the most part, scholars have played the odds and long since rejected the second choice altogether. It is too much to expect, they say, that two highly advanced (in many ways almost identical) cultures could have sprung up at about the same time in different parts of the world. Instead, they have sought ties between America and the long-established "cradle of civilization" in the Middle East—Sumeria, Egypt, Babylonia, Greece, and Persia.

Certainly one of the most fascinating solutions to the problem is to be found among the divers flood legends of the ancient world. Of these, the most familiar to us is the biblical account set forth in the book of Genesis. This is the story of Noah and his ark, which is actually not a single story at all but a blend of two distinct tales of the early Hebrews, and it bears a striking likeness to contemporary Babylonian accounts.

Tales of deluge are also widely found among the peoples of southern Asia. And they have been told by the aborigines of Australia and on the islands of the South Pacific as well.

An Icelandic version traces the flood's origins to the flowing blood of a wounded giant, while a South American tribal tale more typically blames it on the will of the angry god Hurakan. An Aztec epic further relates in some detail the story of a man named Coxcox, a Mexican counterpart of the biblical Noah, through whom the world was saved.

Similarities between American and Hebrew-Baylonian accounts are remarkable: a "darkening" over the land, the quaking of the earth, its rising waters, the terrible noises of the heavens, the panic of the people. But what is truly mysterious is that, so far as history knows, the two ancient cultures of America and the Middle East were completely ignorant of each other's very existence. How, then, could they have produced a similar mythology?

Perhaps, contend some scholars, the story is not mythology at all. Possibly there was just such a terrible deluge, one that destroyed much of the known world. Possibly, too, there were survivors of that deluge. If so, they may eventually have landed on the shores of South America and given rise to or mingled with the Indian cultures later found there. Their discovery of the "New World" would thus have beaten Columbus by a good couple of thousand years.

Atlantists, in particular, hastened to accept the flood theory. The "lost continent," many claimed, was never lost at all; rather, it was pulled—literally pulled—across the Atlantic by that violent storm and permanently relocated.

As early as 1553, the Spanish missionary and historian Francisco López de Gómara wrote that the two continents, Atlantis and South America, were really one and the same. Columbus, he said, had only recently rediscovered that "Island and firm land" which Plato had long ago described.

By the nineteenth century, the thinking of some Atlantists had become a good deal more sophisticated. Hence, the contention of one Robert Prutz, a German historian, that the civilization of Atlantis had found a new home among the Mayas long after its native "Island and firm land" was destroyed in the great deluge. Survivors had been assimilated among an intermediary race, perhaps Phoenician; and it was these latter people who brought about the actual cultural transfer. The Phoenicians, after all, were a sailing people. They might, said Prutz, have made their way through the Red Sea and around the southern tip of Africa, crossing westward then over the South Atlantic.

Non-Atlantists, of course, have scoffed long and hard at such a notion. In his book, *Lost Continents*, Lyon Sprague de Camp sums up their argument. "From the scientific point of view," he says, "it has too many facts against it: that the native American civilizations were barely rising from barbarism in Plato's time; that they never developed the material technics to mount military expeditions across an ocean; that before Plato's time Mediterranean ships could not go across the Atlantic and back. They could not row it because they could not carry enough food and water for the rowers, and they could not sail it because tacking against the wind had not yet been invented."

Mayan civilization, de Camp maintains, was wholly indigenous and, until relatively modern times, fully isolated from European and Middle Eastern influences. Its people thus were racially, linguistically, and culturally unique.

Such reasoning may have been "scientific," but it was not necessarily correct. For at least one recent discovery has lent strong support to Prutz's theory. In 1968, Dr. Cyrus H. Gordon presented tangible proof that Phoenician voyagers may, indeed, have visited the region of the Mayas. And they might have done so, he said, as early as the sixth century B.C., some two hundred years before Plato wrote his account of the destruction of Atlantis.

Dr. Gordon, professor of Near Eastern Studies at Brandeis University, submitted his evidence in the form of an inscribed stone found by a plantation slave in Brazil. It reads, according to the professor's own translation:

> We are Sons of Canaan from Sidon, the city of the king. Commerce has cast us on this distant shore, a land of mountains. We set (sacrificed) a youth for the exalted gods and goddesses in the 19th year of Hiram, our mighty king. We embarked from Ezion-Geber into the Red Sea and voyaged with 10 ships. We were at sea together for two years around the land belonging to Ham (Africa) but were separated by a storm (lit., "from the hand of Baal") and we were no longer with our companions. So we have come here, 12 men and 3 women, on a new shore which I, the Admiral, control. But auspiciously may the exalted gods and goddesses favor us!

The document was actually discovered in 1872, but it had long been taken for a fraud. Its crude lettering and the use of certain words were not considered characteristic of the Phoenicians. Recent studies, however, have led to greater understanding of both the people and their language. And this, in turn, has tended to corroborate the accuracy of the stone's inscription—all the more so since this newly gained knowledge could not have been available to any would-be forger as long as 100 years ago.

Not even Dr. Gordon, though, would deign to rob Columbus of his glory. But that glory, he says, rests upon the Italian explorer's success in opening up vast new regions to European commerce—not on his discovery of any "New World."

American civilizations, he insists, were repeatedly visited—and probably strongly influenced in their development—by foreigners for thousands of years before the *Nina, Pinta,* and *Santa Maria* ever set sail across the wide waters of the Atlantic.

And it may yet turn out that the venerable Donnelly was on the right track all along with his reconstruction of man's prehistory. "Atlantis and the western continent," he wrote in 1882, "had from an immemorial age held intercourse with each other; the great nations of America were simply colonies from Atlantis, sharing in its civilization, language, religion, and blood. From Mexico to the peninsula of Yucatan, from the shores of Brazil to the heights of Bolivia and Peru, from the Gulf of Mexico to the headwaters of the Mississippi River, the colonies of Atlantis extended."

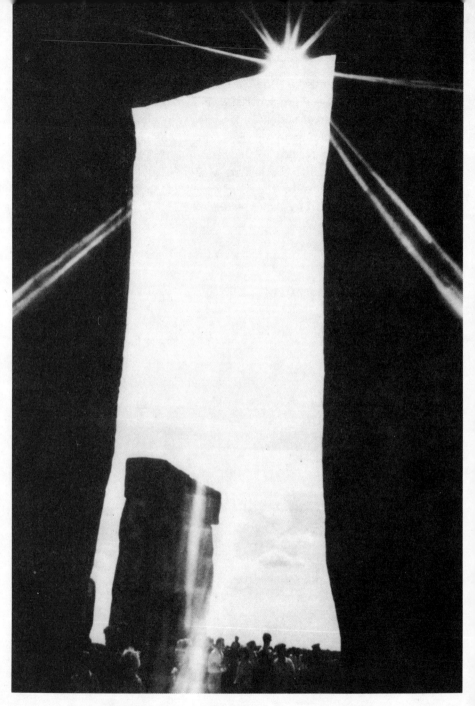

Visitors at Stonehenge.—*Photograph by the author*

DANCE
OF
THE
GIANTS

---

*the
mystery
of
the
Stonehenge ruins...*

VIEWED FROM THE air during early morning, it seems desolate and gaunt—a tiny cluster of stones there on the barren plain like building blocks the children might have left out in the sandbox overnight. For this is Stonehenge, silent remnant of another age and a reminder of man's beginnings.

Seen from ground level, the ruins lose that strange solemnity. Gone is the perspective of time and space; gone, too, the silence of it all. By midday, long lines of tourists gather for admission. They've come to see more than the relic of a bygone civilization. They've come to explore a living legend.

For this is Stonehenge, sadly neglected over the years but not forgotten. Its mystery lingers to taunt us still. What manner of ancient man would want to build so curious a monument? And why? And how would he have gone about it without our modern implements?

For centuries, the tribal lore of old Britain provided history with the color, if not the truth, of Stonehenge. The earliest claimed it was a temple erected by the medieval wizard Merlin to commemorate noble British warriors slain on that spot by the Saxon host.

"If thou be fain," he said, according to the illustrious twelfth-century bishop, Geoffrey of Monmouth, "to grace the burial-place of these men with a work that shall endure forever, send for the Dance of the Giants that is in Killaraus, a mountain in Ireland. For a structure of stones is there that none of this age could raise save his wit were strong enough to carry his art. For the stones be big, nor is there stone anywhere of more virtue, and, so they be set up round this plot in a circle, even as they be now there set up, here shall they stand for ever."

Curiously, Merlin was said to have used earthly powers, not magical, to transport those stones to the construction site. This would indicate perhaps that some memory of the moving process lingered on among the traditions of Geoffrey's day. (In 1954, the British Broadcasting Company sponsored a venture in which four schoolboys poled prehistoric-style canoes upriver, against the current of the Avon, and proved that the heavy slabs of stone *could* have been floated down from as far away as South Wales.)

The Merlin theory began losing favor during the fifteenth century, when the anonymous author of the *Chronicle of England* stated for a fact that there was no connection between the medieval wizard and the building of Stonehenge. For the next hundred years, popular opinion ran all the more strongly against the possibility—except among romantics like Edmund Spenser, who assured Geoffrey's tale a lease on life by its inclusion in his classic *The Faerie Queene*.

But it remained for the seventeenth century to produce an alternative theory of any great appeal. This one was advanced by John Aubrey. In addition to his fame as the author of *Brief Lives* (and not too large or lasting a fame at that), Aubrey was also something of an archeologist. At least, he was the closest anyone had come in English history to being a real student of that particular science.

He was also well known in contemporary social circles as a personal friend of King Charles II. In 1663, Charles commissioned him to study the Stonehenge structure and the diverse stories of its origins.

"There have been several Books writt by learned men concerning Stoneheng," Aubrey noted in his journal, "much differing from one another, some affirming one thing, some another. Now I come in the Rear of all by comparative Arguments to give a clear evidence these monuments were Pagan Temples; which was not made-out before: and have also, with humble submission to better judgements, offered a probability, that they were Temples of the Druids. . . . This Inquiry, I must confess, is a gropeing in the Dark; but although I have not brought it into a clear light; yet I can affirm that I have brought it from an utter darkness to a thin mist, and have gonne further in this Essay than any one before me. These Antiquities are so exceedingly old that no Bookes doe reach them, so that there is no Way to retrive them but by comparative antiquitie, which I have writt upon the spott, from the Monuments themselves. Historia quoquo modo scripta, bona est [In whatever way history is written, it is good]."

Aubrey's history was good enough to fire the imagination of his countrymen as none had ever done before. And it was some three hundred years before the notion of Druids could generally be put to rest. In some quarters, it persists yet.

That there were Druids is a matter of historical record. They were the holy men of the Celts. They were the priests, the teachers, even the judges among them. In his account of the Gallic Wars, Julius Caesar noted that the nobility of all Gaul was divided into two parts: Druids and knights. "The former," he explained, "officiate at divine worship, regulate sacrifices public and private, and expound questions of ritual." It is true, too, that these Druids inhabited Britain, even possible that they made use of the strange and mystical Stonehenge in their practices. But it is doubtful that they were the ones who built the monument or that they even set foot on British soil until after it was built.

Twentieth-century diggings have yielded reliable evidence that the ruins of Stonehenge date, not from Roman times, but from as far back as the New Stone and Bronze ages. They are nearly as old, then, as the pyramids of Egypt, older than the rubble of fallen Troy.

Nor, most likely, was Stonehenge built all at once. It was constructed, it seems, in three stages, beginning as early as the days of Abraham. Completion extended over a period of several centuries, probably from about 2000 to nearly 1400 B.C.

The first of these stages was the simplest both in plan and execution. A ditch was dug some 400 feet in diameter, encircling an inner bank that was covered with solid chalk. The bank rose higher than the level of earth outside the ditch, which itself is notable inasmuch as it is contrary to the usual design of ancient British monuments.

Just inside the ditch, also completely surrounding that inner bank, 56 holes were dug from two to four feet deep and from two and a half to six feet wide. These were irregularly spaced around the rim of the inner bank and later filled in.

The holes never held any posts. They were not dug as graves, although corpses were later found in them. One can only guess that they were of some spiritual value. They have since been named for John Aubrey, who discovered them and mapped their location during the course of his survey after they had been obscured by millennia of disuse.

It was this same Aubrey who named the fourth landmark of that first Stonehenge period. This was the heelstone, so called because Aubrey insisted he had seen in it the imprint of a "Friar's heel." No such imprint has ever been observed by anyone else, but the name remains.

Standing as it does 100 feet outside the perimeter of the regular structure and surrounded by a ditch of its own, this lone rock presumably had special significance to the monument's builders. Indeed, it may have been the key to their grand design. It stands today like a stone iceberg—a 35-ton, 1,000-cubic-foot mass sunk 4 feet into the ground, oddly separated from the main body of Stonehenge yet somehow an integral part ot it.

This first phase, or Stonehenge I as scholars know it, probably took Neolithic man several decades to complete. About two centuries after he was done, his successors resumed the task.

These were the Beaker people, who got their name from a quaint habit of burying drinking vessels with the dead. In many ways, the Beakers were the most sophisticated men of the Stone Age; and their assets ranged far beyond their skill in the making of pottery. For one thing, they were accomplished builders. For another, they'd been around.

They were traveling folk who had come mostly from Holland and the Rhineland and settled in eastern Britain. And, all along the way, they had established continuing trade routes. One of these followed the west coast of Wales into the Bristol Channel, whence came the Pembrokeshire blue-stones that characterized the monument's second phase.

During Stonehenge II, no fewer than eighty of these blue-stones were set up in a double circle well inside the perimeter of the Aubrey holes. At the same time, the Avenue was laid out, leading past the old heelstone and on about three-tenths of a mile before bending eastward to the River Avon.

The pattern of this second phase was never completed, however. Some stones were never set into the holes dug for them; some holes were only partially dug. Why the Beaker men stopped just short of their apparent goal is not known. But it is interesting that the end of their labors also marked the end of the Stone Age in Britain.

Then along came the Wessex people with another idea.

Whether the Wessex were an invading force who settled in the vicinity, or whether they were simply an assimilated and advanced version of the Beakers, has never been fully determined. Nor does it matter much. What is important is that they were the locally dominant force at the beginning of the Bronze Age. It was they who inaugurated the last phase of building in about 1500 B.C.

They had already developed a highly organized culture, one that could boast an intricate power structure and a strong economy based on craftsmanship, farming, and commerce. They were clustered into separate tribes, each led by a warrior chieftain. But there was relatively little fighting either among the tribes or with outside forces. They had direct access to much of the world beyond Britain—but almost entirely for the peaceful purposes of trading.

In fact, says one leading British archeologist, R. J. C. Atkinson, it was probably through their dealings abroad that the Wessex obtained the services of the true architect of Stonehenge III. He points out a heavy Mediterranean in-fluence on the monument's design as well as the presence of

Mediterranean artifacts and carvings found among the burials there. Moreover, he says, there is nothing else in all of Britain that is anything like Stonehenge. To have constructed so complex an arrangement, the native population would have needed experience; and that kind of experience would surely have involved actual prototypes, of which none has ever been found.

"It seems to me," writes Atkinson, "that to account for these exotic and unparalleled features one *must* assume the existence of influence from the only contemporary European cultures in which *architecture,* as distinct from mere construction, was already a living tradition; that is, from the Mycenaean and Minoan civilizations of the central Mediterranean."

The construction itself was probably carried out in three separate stages, lasting a total of about a hundred years.

First came dismantling of the bluestones erected during Stonehenge II. These were laid to one side for later use. In their stead, the Wessex raised a circle of sarsen stone, and inside that a horseshoe of the same. In both cases, the stones were fitted into trilithons, two upright units capped with a crosspiece or lintel to form a stone archway. There were five such trilithons in the horseshoe, thirty in the circle around it.

Next, twenty of the bluestones were selected and carefully shaped for placement in a horseshoe within the sarsen horseshoe. To accommodate the remainder, a double circle of holes (now labeled Y and Z) was dug outside the sarsen circle itself.

But the job was never finished. Perhaps some calamity—martial, natural, or otherwise—interrupted their work and indefinitely postponed it. Perhaps the builders simply changed their minds about the scheme they had undertaken. The halt is but one of many minor mysteries connected with the building of Stonehenge.

In any case, by the time the Wessex got back to work only a few years later, they had decided to do without the bluestone horseshoe. The remaining sixty bluestones were brought back inside the sarsens and massed with the others in a closely spaced circle.

Thus, from the first, the basic shape of Stonehenge was obvious. The Aubrey-holes circle, the sarsen circle, the Y- and Z-holes circles, the bluestone circle—all these accounted for more than 500 years of building on the site. Presumably, there was some purpose to it all.

What interests us about Stonehenge is not so much that it exists, though its physical presence is certainly impressive. What interests us is *why* it exists.

The project, after all, took half a millennium to bring to completion. It required, according to one recent calculation, no fewer than 1½ million man-days of labor. (That's more than 40 men working around the clock for 100 years.) It required the ingenuity to transport those heavy stones over land and sea for distances of hundreds of miles. It required the expenditure of a large portion of community wealth that might well have been spent otherwise.

An interesting estimate of comparative cost has been put forth by the well-known astronomy professor Gerald S. Hawkins. "The [U.S.] Space Program," he says, "takes about one per cent of our gross national product; Stonehenge must have taken at least a corresponding amount. Their building effort may have required more of them than our Space Program does of us; correspondingly, it could have meant much more to them."

Obviously, though, it meant much more than the sacrifice of money and manpower alone. It involved a sense of purpose, a dedication, that could not be eroded by the passage of time. It was a virtual obsession.

Was it worth the cost? If so, why? Was Stonehenge built merely as a testimonial to the prowess of ancient man? Or did it serve some larger purpose?

What, in short, does Stonehenge mean?

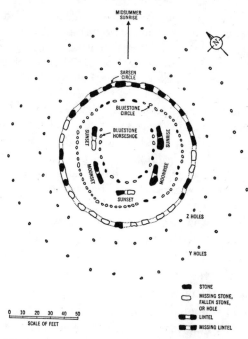

Stonehenge III.—*From* Stonehenge Decoded *by Gerald S. Hawkins. Copyright © 1965 by Gerald S. Hawkins and John B. White. Reproduced by permission of Doubleday & Company, Inc.*

As long ago as 1771, a physician named John Smith pointed out the curious alignment of the heelstone to the midsummer sunrise. Thus, he noted, on the longest day of the year, one can stand in the center of the monument and watch the sun come up directly over that large, isolated stone. But Smith's contemporaries considered it nothing more than coincidence —if, indeed, they considered it at all.

Succeeding generations clung to their doubts. No self-respecting scientist, it seemed, wanted to admit that this kind of intellectual planning could have been possible.

Then, in 1961, Professor Hawkins called on computers to do the job that scholars themselves had shunned for nearly two full centuries:

First we put charts of Stonehenge into "Oscar," a plotting machine that transforms positions into X, Y coordinates on punched cards. Then we fed those coordinates into the Harvard-Smithsonian IBM 7090 computer and asked it to calculate azimuths, or compass directions, determined by some 170 pairs of positions, a position being a stone, stone hole, mound, archway, or the center. Next we asked the machine to translate those azimuths into declinations, that is, to determine the "latitudes" of the celestial sphere they intersected.

Then we examined those declinations, the horizon spots to which the Stonehenge pairs pointed. Was there any pattern to them? Did the pairs point to significant rise or set positions of celestial bodies?

The answer was yes. As he had suspected from the start, Hawkins found a probable correlation of many of these pairs with the motion of the sun. But he also found, much to his surprise, an even more frequent matching of pairs with various positions of the moon. And since the relative motion of the moon is a good deal more complicated than that of the sun, any such lunar orientation of Stonehenge seemed all the more strange.

In short order, Hawkins fed additional data into the computers. These included the relative positions of those same celestial bodies, not as they are today but as they were in the year 1500 B.C. The findings of this survey were even more telling than the first.

In all, the computers located ten solar and fourteen lunar correlations:

It is important to note that *all* of the twenty-four alignments are between key positions—the center of the structure, the "avenue" or most important axis, the great trilithon arches; the rectangle of "stations," the uniquely-placed stones near the entrance. Every one of these key positions paired with others to point to a sun or moon rise or set. That solidly establishes the fact that those alignments were significant, deliberate, basic in the construction. Stonehenge lived by the sun and moon.

But why?

Was Stonehenge constructed as an astronomical observatory, pure and simple? If it was, then for what purpose? To note the change of seasons? To predict eclipses?

It would be hard to account for such sophistication of purpose among the primitive tribesmen of ancient Britain. Moreover, given that sophistication, it would seem incredible that succeeding generations should have lost it and not been able in modern times to comprehend what marvel had been wrought there.

Or perhaps all the technological implications we now at last perceive never fully occurred to the builders of that great monument. Perhaps they meant, instead, to erect a kind of shrine—a temple only roughly aligned to both sun and moon —the main purposes of which were to attract divine guidance for the people of the tribes and to enhance the mystical powers of their priests.

Or, put another way, did the people of Stonehenge ever really know themselves just what it was that they had built?

The twin sciences of astronomy and computer processing can give us insight into the mechanics of these ancient ruins. But revelations are not solutions. And the more we have revealed to us of the nature of Stonehenge, the more tantalizing becomes the ultimate mystery: not what was Stonehenge, after all, but *why* was Stonehenge?

We may never know for sure.

YETI

---

the
legend
of
the
Abominable Snowman...

HE'S BEEN CALLED the "missing link." Half-man, half-beast.

He's huge, maybe as much as eight feet tall. His body is covered with long brown hair. He has a pointed head, and his face is hairless and looks rather like a man's face. He walks upright. And he lives near the top of the highest mountain in the world.

He's the Abominable Snowman, and he's either the product of an overworked imagination or the strangest creature on the face of the earth!

Of course, the legend of the Snowman has been around for quite some time. Among the Sherpa natives of the Himalayas it is centuries old. But it was only as recently as 1921 that it made its way deep into Western lore.

That was the year an English colonel, Howard Bury, started out on a daring expedition to scale Mount Everest. Bury, a former battalion commander in the Sixtieth Rifles, had spent years in Central Asia. He had become especially familiar with that border terrain between India and Tibet and was an experienced climber. He was well prepared to lead this assault.

The fact that he failed did not lessen the importance of his effort. For he and his men made a curious discovery along the way.

"We distinguished hare and fox tracks," he wrote of his adventure, "but one mark, like that of a human foot, was most puzzling. The coolies assured us that it was the track of a wild, hairy man, and these men were occasionally to be found in the wildest and most inaccessible mountains."

News of the discovery spread fast. It gripped the public fancy with all the intensity of the incredible. It *was* incredible. Yet men would spend decades thereafter, risk life and limb, consume fortunes to locate just such a "wild, hairy man" as Bury reported living among snowy peaks in that rarefied air some 15,000 to 20,000 feet above sea level. It became something of an explorer's obsession.

Endless stories were told of natives having sighted the

precious *Yeti*, as they called their Snowman. And a Nepalese government official related the previous capture of two specimens on separate occasions.

The first, he said, was an infant *Yeti*, or "snowbaby," as journalists would dub it. A group of roving Sherpas came upon him in broad daylight; but, by the time their messenger got back with a party equipped to trap the creature, those natives had disappeared along with their prize. None was ever seen again.

Capture of an adult male was also reported. In this case, though, the bound prisoner brooded throughout the long trip down the slopes, refused to eat, and finally starved to death. His ignorant captors simply abandoned the carcass en route.

Skeptics, needless to say, found it easy to scoff at the stories. No one had ever really seen the creature. At least, no "reliable" witness could be found. Some claimed he was a nocturnal being, but this provided no more than a convenient excuse. And, in any case, he lived at such heights that few could even get close to him day or night.

Not only that, but who or what could live at those heights on which this *Yeti* might feed? One really ingenious soul suggested that the Snowman probably ate something called "ice worms." The female of the species, or Snowoman, possibly ate Snowmen as well.

The legend of the *Yeti* gradually dissolved into a joke. It made good copy for the press on a slow news day. It offered an exotic setting for science fiction movies. It was fun, but highly unreal.

Then, in 1951, an explorer named Eric Shipton made an unusual find in the snows of Everest. This was a set of tracks he guessed could only have been made by a real Snowman. They were fresh tracks. They were gigantic. And he brought back pictures to prove it!

Shipton had been scouting for an alternative route climbers might use to ascend the mighty Everest. A few parties had come close over the years, but none had ever quite made it all the way to the top. It was Shipton's job to determine if another, more feasible path existed than that by which so many had already failed. It was while he was crossing one of the glaciers of the Menlung basin on the south face of the mountain that he first noticed the tracks. At that point, the Shipton party stood 19,000 feet above sea level.

It was late afternoon. Soon the sun would set. Quickly he got to work recording his find on film as he and the men with him followed those tracks for more than a mile.

"I have in the past," he observed, "found many sets of these curious footprints and have tried to follow them, but have always lost them on the moraine or rocks at the side of the glacier. These particular ones seemed to be very fresh, probably not more than 24 hours old."

The track was monstrously large. It was every bit as long as the bar of a climber's pick that had been laid alongside it for comparison in one of Shipton's many photographs. And it clearly showed that, where the animal had jumped across a wide crevice in the glacier, it had dug its toes deep into the snow to keep from falling. Yet, there was something curious about the position of the toes. They were actually the closest to the edge of any part of the track. It was as if the creature had put his feet on backwards!

Shipton left the slopes some time later, convinced that Snowmen might really exist. He would not believe that such tracks as these could have been made by anything known to man—not any kind of monkey or Himalayan red bear. The monkey and the bear were two of the most widely accepted "explanations" of the phenomenon at the time.

The explorer's conviction was shared by fellow-adventurer Edmund Hillary. A New Zealand beekeeper by profession, Hillary made a name for himself in 1953 when he led the victorious summit party of an Everest expedition under Sir John Hunt. The feat was a remarkable one, and it earned Hillary a knighthood from the queen. It also stimulated him to further quest.

Thus, seven years later, the climber, now Sir Edmund, went back to Everest for the sequel to his first success.

As the *New York Times* reported, "Mr. Hillary, according to his friends, had two life-long ambitions—to be the first to conquer Mt. Everest and to capture one of the 'abominable snowmen' reputed to inhabit the icy slopes of the world's highest mountain. He said before he left Auckland to join the expedition he was convinced the 'abominable snowmen' were no myth."

Other explorers, meanwhile, had already tried their luck. One of them was a Texas oilman and rancher named Tom Slick. During 1957 and 1958, Slick's party made two prolonged forays among the snowy peaks to seek out the elusive *Yeti*.

At least, that was the party's stated intention. They traveled under the banner of the San Antonio Zoological Society, which maintained a purely scientific interest in the search. But spokesmen for various Communist governments in Eastern Europe and in Asia envisaged an entirely different purpose.

Espionage charges were hurled furiously. "A dispatch from Peiping," noted an American foreign correspondent, "warned that searching parties now 'intensively reconnoitering' the China-Nepal border resembled dangerous missions once sent to snoop around the Soviet-Turkish frontier in search of Noah's Ark."

The snooping, though, paid off in exciting ways. The Slick party photographed some fresh tracks of its own; they even brought back strands of hair thought to be those of the Snowman. Subsequent examination by experts bore out the possibility, noting that the animal in question wasn't related to monkeys or bears.

French, Swiss, and British parties also combed the area. One of these, the so-called *Daily Mail* Expedition out of London, was chronicled by Ralph Izzard, a member of the group. He concluded that the *Yeti* really existed and that he was a creature altogether new to science. He thrived on insects, mouse-rabbits, and other small mammals that were able to live at those high altitudes. His size was probably only that of a boy in his early teens; and he sometimes went about on all fours, although often he would walk erect. He had no tail, and his body was covered with reddish brown hair.

"Few of us who have gone into this matter of the Snowman's credentials," Izzard concluded, "will not agree with Colonel Hunt when he says that sufficient reliable evidence now exists to warrant the organization of an expedition founded on a proper scientific basis and charged with the sole objective of proving or disproving his existence."

It was Hunt's erstwhile colleague, Sir Edmund Hillary, who came close to doing just that in 1960. Actually, the New Zealander's party was organized primarily to test the ability of the human body to survive in such thin, high-altitude atmosphere. They would climb high into the Himalayas, from 15,000 to 19,000 feet above sea level, and try to live there for about six months. During all that time, they would make every effort to locate the *Yeti*.

Ideally, they would capture one alive. In any event, they were equipped to photograph him from great distances and to record the weird whistling or hissing cry attributed to him. At the very least, they hoped to observe a single specimen through powerful field glasses.

They never did, though. The only substantive signs of the Snowman were still more footprints. And by then Hillary had seen quite enough footprints. What's more, he had also begun to develop strong doubts about these. Probably, he felt, they were nothing more than ordinary animal tracks—foxes, snow leopards, wolves, bears—that had been greatly enlarged in the sun's daily thawing of the snow and preserved by the cold nights between.

Another bit of evidence, a so-called *Yeti* scalp, was subsequently found to be a fake. Hillary had borrowed it from a Nepalese monastery, where it had been kept for as long as anyone could remember. He had it examined by experts in London, Paris, and Chicago. All agreed that it was old, perhaps more than 100 years old. But it was definitely not a scalp of any kind. It was a cap molded from the skin of a serow, or long-haired goat.

What it all came down to, then, was a matter of faith. And Sir Edmund was fast losing his. There was no scientific proof to encourage further support. All that remained was the word of those witnesses who claimed actually to have seen a *Yeti.* Not many had.

The stately *New York Times* ran the story of Hillary's disenchantment on its society page under the succinct headline: SNOWMAN MELTED.

Yet, no sooner did the case seem closed than it was suddenly reopened. In February, 1964, Boris F. Porshnev, a member of the Soviet Academy of Sciences, announced that he had long been investigating the matter himself. His conclusions fairly shocked Western colleagues.

This Snowman, he said, was very likely a surviving remnant of Neanderthal man (the prehistoric ancestor of *homo sapiens* that dominated what is now Western Europe from about 25,000 to 75,000 years ago). The Russian scholar would not disclose the evidence on which his case rested. But there had long been hints of Russian interest in the mystery—despite all the derision and protests regarding Western investigations.

One account, published in the *New York Times,* recounted the examination of a captured specimen by a Soviet army doctor during World War II. Apparently, Red soldiers in the Himalayas thought they had a naked enemy agent on their hands. But the "suspect" was extremely hairy, and he perspired so during the indoor examination that he had to be taken back out into the wintry cold to restore him to normality. Results of that study and the events that followed it have never been revealed. But one hopes the creature some-how escaped execution as a spy!

During the International Geophysical Year of 1957-58, Leningrad University Professor A. G. Pronin disclosed that he had twice seen what seemed to be a Snowman. He had made his observations, he explained, while climbing in the Pamir Mountains of Central Asia. His own colleagues scoffed at the assertion; and fellow scientists in the West thought so little of Pronin's story that they completely ignored it in their own later writings and discussions.

Nine months later, though, a distinguished team of Russian scientists and historians acknowledged that they had really taken the Pronin account quite seriously. During the interim they had studied not only the professor's report but also a number of previous reports on the Snowman. Strangely enough, they said, the existence of such a creature was actu-ally being "confirmed little by little."

It is interesting to note that this team was headed by the historian Boris F. Porshnev, the same Boris F. Porshnev who six years later would put forth the hypothesis of the Neander-thal man. What transpired in the course of those years cannot be fully known. But it was publicly announced at the time of the 1958 report that the team would start a special Soviet collective near the border of Tibet and Northwest China. The purpose of that collective, it was further stated, was not to catch a *Yeti* but to study native reports and to gather evidence of scientific value.

"The 'catching' will come in time," the scientists agreed, "but only as a result of persistent and serious accumulation and analysis of various data."

Whether the Neanderthal theory was founded on such analysis cannot be deduced. Nor have we any idea just what data have been accumulated in the years since then. But it is clear that these men of science, at least, continue to take the legend of the Snowman seriously. And it's a good bet that, as long as the Russians are interested, Western scientists are going to maintain some interest of their own.

So the mystery goes on, Sir Edmund notwithstanding. And if some day there is, indeed, a "catching" of the *Yeti*, then a curious dilemma once cited by that famous climber may yet confront the catchers:

"As one Chicago pundit put the problem, Do you book it into the Palmer House or into the Lincoln Park Zoo?"

A photograph of the Loch Ness monster taken by Dr. Robert Kenneth Wilson.—*Photograph courtesy Wide World Photos*

HIGHLAND FLING

---

*the
search
for
the
Loch Ness monster...*

BOBBY WAS "BORN" in 1933. But his story goes back more than a thousand years. He is Scotland's oldest, most baffling legend.

It was on May 22 that John McKay and his wife were out driving along the north shore of Loch Ness. The road was a new one, finished just that spring. And construction hands who worked on it had recently reported strange stirrings in the waters of the loch. But it was the McKays who chanced to locate the cause of those mysterious movements.

Suddenly, out of nowhere, there loomed a creature such as they had never seen before. It was huge and terrifying. And it traveled at great speed, disappearing quickly into the loch.

Their story brought to mind older tales of a terrible Loch Ness monster. These date as far back as the era of St. Columba, Abbot of Iona. In the year 565, it is said, the abbot used the power of prayer to drive off the menace of a "water monster" there.

The beast was preparing to attack a defenseless swimmer. But Columba called to it, saying, "Think not to go further nor touch thou that man. Quick go back!"

As it happened, the good saint had a powerful voice; and the loudness of his prayer might have helped considerably.

Reports of a "water horse" or "dark monster" continued throughout the Middle Ages. The creature closely resembled the one the abbot had faced, but it was never again said to be the least bit aggressive. As a matter of fact, it seemed rather timid.

In recent centuries, however, the beast was rarely seen. And the legend became an incident of ancient history—at least until construction in 1933 of a highway from Inverness to Fort Augustus. This was the road the McKays took late that spring. By the end of the year, no fewer than 155 people claimed to have seen the monster. Yet, in every case, the slightest sound or movement sent it scurrying back into the depths of the loch. All the observers steadfastly denied the possibility of an optical illusion.

Local Scotsmen fondly dubbed the monster Bobby. They considered him something of a community pet and protested sharply the dangerous influx of curiosity-seeking tourists. They protested so sharply, in fact, that the country's secretary of state issued an official warning that "the creature, if sighted, must not on any pretext be molested, shot or trapped."

Not that Bobby wasn't big enough to take care of himself. Reports varied as to his size, but only slightly. All seemed to agree that the creature was gigantic.

"An abomination," one of the first observers called him, "with a three-arched neck and a body four feet high." Others described him as "monstrously large" and "terribly powerful." One noted that he "lashed the water into a turmoil" in the course of a swift departure.

A veterinary student saw the creature from his motorcycle. He said it had a "hefty" body, with two front flippers and two others behind, seemingly webbed. Its total length, he said, was fifteen to twenty feet, including a tail about five feet long. An Inverness chemist was most impressed with its huge neck and strong, thrashing tail.

Two passing officers of the Scottish Autocycle Union "could see distinctly two humps and a smallish head and its skin seemed rough like an elephant's."

A composite picture thus emerged of a long, large beast with a humped back, a swanlike neck, and a flat but disproportionately small head. The tail was long and quite strong.

Despite his size, the animal was anything but aggressive. Whenever sighted, he was either swimming peacefully along in the calm loch waters or basking on stones near the shore. He always retreated from view at the first sign of passers-by.

The monster's bashfulness did not entirely prevent observation, however. One witness reported having spent fifteen minutes or so quietly watching it loll about at the water's edge. Another, Dr. Robert Kenneth Wilson, a highly respected surgeon on the staff of the London Hospital, had time to get out his photographic gear and shoot four pictures of the creature.

"When I saw the head of the strange animal rising up out of the water," he explained, "I was so excited I did not pause to observe it properly. Instead, I dashed for the camera. . . ."

Unfortunately for science, the doctor's photographs were made at a distance of about 200 yards. The results, therefore, were something less than conclusive.

Inconclusive, too, were the results of a massive observation project organized by Sir Edward Mountain in July, 1934. Sir Edward recruited more than twenty part-time watchers to await Bobby's next appearance. Together they accounted for ten man-weeks of effort, ever at the ready with cameras, field glasses, and note pads to record the monster's moves.

But the monster proved painfully uncooperative. He showed up only once, very late in the season; and, at that, he managed to be some three-quarters of a mile from the nearest observer. Motion pictures shot from that vantage point, even aided by the use of a telephoto lens, produced images too small for positive identification. But they led some people to speculate nonetheless that the animal was merely a large gray seal that had somehow strayed from its native saltwater habitat.

The curator of mammals at the London Zoo did not agree. He had earlier reached a similar conclusion on the basis of other information. But the Wilson photographs completely changed his mind.

"This puts an end," he said, "to my theory that the Loch Ness Monster was a grey seal. It is certainly not a seal. If it [a photograph] had been taken from the deck of a liner in mid-ocean, I should have said it was a sea serpent, but it is impossible to believe such a monster could have entered the fresh water of the loch."

That fresh water runs 24 miles through the beautiful Great Glen of the Scottish Highlands. The loch is approximately 750 feet deep and, at its widest point, a mile and a half across.

Its closest link with the sea is the Caledonian Canal. For a creature of Bobby's size to have entered through the canal—or to have managed some narrow river passage from either the North Sea or the Atlantic—is highly improbable. Chances are that, if he existed at all, he was every inch as much a native of the region as the people of Inverness whose shores he graced so guardedly during those years 1933 and 1934.

Twenty-five years earlier, an animal very similar to Bobby had been spotted in Sweden. Townfolk there nicknamed that one Storsjoodjuretuppenbarelserna, in honor of the lake in which he dwelt. "Let it be said emphatically, now and here," commented the *Quarterly Review*, an eminently respectable English journal, at the time, "that to a mind that is ready to learn, there is no reason whatever to doubt the occasional, and by-no-means infrequent, appearance, not only in the great ocean and in the smaller seas, but even estuaries, lochs and fjords, of huge marine monsters, unknown to science and unclassified."

The director of the Zoological Society's aquarium in London expressed similar thoughts about Bobby. And the Right Reverend David Hunter Blair, Abbot of Dunfermline, Scotland, went so far as to speculate in *The Commonweal* that the animal belonged to the postglacial period when all the Lochs Ness, Oich, and Lochy were still connected with the ocean.

The suggestion by a medical student who had seen the creature went a bit further. "It looks like a hybrid," he said, "something between a plesiosaurus and the seal tribe."

Seal tribes didn't generate much excitement, but the possibility of a prehistoric monster gave the Loch Ness mystery added dimension. The plesiosaurus, after all, was an ideal candidate. For the most part, he was reasonably gentle, defensive, fish-eating, and equally at home in fresh and salt water.

It is important to note the seriousness with which this possibility was taken by many contemporary scientists. Even those who did not accept it felt compelled to dispute it in public precisely because they recognized its viability. One of these was the prominent marine biologist, Dr. William Beebe, who wanted it put on record quite simply and in all seriousness that "in all my deep-sea work I have found no living relics of the past, no simple forms, no preservation of past life."

Beebe's own guess was that the creature was a giant squid, whereas the director emeritus of the Berlin Zoo called it a killer whale. Others were less generous.

"It's not a problem for zoologists but for psychologists," said Sir Arthur Keith, one of England's foremost anthropologists. So saying, he sounded the keynote for subsequent consideration of the phenomenon. The seriousness was slowly dissipated. Legend turned to fable; the fable became a joke.

During the years since 1934, there have been relatively few sightings of the creature. But every summer Inverness-shire, the county of Inverness, is crowded with tourists ready to have a go at it. It's called the "silly season," that time of year. And even most visitors admit to the nonsense of their trip. They've come on a lark.

(Local merchants bitterly resent the charge that they created the myth in the first place just to lure this tourist trade. But they admit the story hasn't hurt business any.)

A dogged few remain convinced of the monster's reality. In 1962, they organized what they called the Loch Ness Phenomena Investigation Bureau, Ltd. The bureau, located in Inverness, is made up of scientists and others trying to identify the creature and chart its behavior patterns.

Whether the result of some really detailed sighting or simply as a sign of growing fondness, they've since endowed the creature with references of the feminine gender. And they call her Nessie now.

"She's my Moby Dick," says the bureau's resident technician, Clem Lister Skelton. In a 1967 interview with a reporter for the Associated Press, Skelton claimed eight sightings of his own. "But the chances of sighting her are not very good. We've averaged a sighting for every 350 man-hours of watching over the past five years. Of course, we're not sure if we always see the same one." There might, he added, be as many as thirty Nessies in the loch.

The project, which costs some $10,000 a year, is financed through private sources. But it has received solid support of quite another sort in military quarters.

Early in 1966, a team of photo-reconnaissance experts for the Royal Air Force and the Defense Ministry studied a 16-mm film clip purporting to show the monster in motion. In a 1,500-word report, they reached "the conclusion that it is probably an animate object." Whatever it is, the report went on, it is about 92 feet long, 6 feet wide, and 5 feet high. And it was moving at the time of the filming at a rate of about 10 miles per hour.

Publication of that report signaled a new round of interest in the investigations. Foremost among latter-day recruits is Dr. Roy Mackal, biochemistry professor at the University of Chicago. "For too long," he complained, "the Loch Ness Monster has been the subject of ridicule, but the people who scoff at it obviously haven't read the evidence."

In 1967, Dr. Mackal secured a grant from Field Enterprises Educational Corporation for an extended surveillance program to garner still more evidence. That program included sonar detection—based on work undertaken by English scientists at the University of Birmingham suggesting that the loch contains some sort of animal life—and the launching of a midget yellow submarine in the summer of 1969.

The search will go on, of course. But for what nobody really knows.

A prehistoric beast? Perhaps. Mackal won't rule out the chances of it. But, meanwhile, he's got his own pet theory: "I think it is closely related to the gastropod family. I think it is a great sea slug."

That in itself would be startling news, however, since the sea slug is only a kind of giant snail. And the largest ever found measured no more than eighteen inches long. Hardly a monster of the deep!

Reading Notes

EXTENSIVE USE WAS made of the *New York Times* and the London *Times* in preparing many of these chapters. Any reader interested in studying further one of the more recent mysteries included in this collection might consult these sources as much to "experience" history as to research it.

Other periodical references are noted in the context of those chapters to which they pertain.

NAKED AGAINST THE NIGHT
The Mysterious Death of Dag Hammarskjold

Known details of the Hammarskjold tragedy are carefully compiled in a U.N. publication that goes by the rather uncompelling title, *Documents A/5069 and Add. 1* (New York, April, 1962). These relate the methods and conclusions of investigations by the U.N. commission assigned to study the death of the Secretary General; reports of the Rhodesian Board of Investigation and Commission of Inquiry; statements of witnesses; maps, charts, and wreckage plans. The details are put into marvelous perspective by Arthur L. Gavshon, whose *The Mysterious Death of Dag Hammarskjold* (New York, 1962) examines the political circumstances surrounding Hammarskjold's Congo visit and their possible implications. Hammarskjold's local emissary, Conor Cruise O'Brien, has himself produced a colorful account that is highly charged with political insight and historical relevance. Emery Kelen's biography, *Hammarskjold* (New York, 1966), provides important background material in addition to a brief review and appraisal of the Secretary General's violent death. The mystery of the man himself, the intellectual foundation and pursuits of his life, these are reflected in the pages of *Markings* (New York, 1964), his own posthumously published book of prayers, verse, and other short writings. The book tells nothing of the ultimate tragedy, of course, but it is a "must" for any reader who would understand and appreciate the man.

WHO KILLED SIR EDMUND?
The "Perfect" Murder of Judge Godfrey

The Murder of Sir Edmund Godfrey was published by the mystery writer John Dickson Carr in 1936 (London). It remains the first line of modern inquiry. The book is an admirable reconstruction of the era of Charles II and a careful collation of data pertaining to the so-called popish plot and the murder that may have come of that intrigue. A shorter inquiry, less comprehensive in scope and in purpose, is offered as part of *The Valet's Tragedy* (London, New York, and Bombay, 1903) by Andrew Lang. The first account of the mysterious death dates back to 1688, with publication of the official *A Brief History of the Times* (London) by the king's historian, Sir Roger L'Estrange. Subsequent histories and biographies include:

Browning, Andrew. *Memoirs of Sir John Reresby*. Glasgow: 1936.
Bryant, Arthur. *King Charles II*. London: 1955.
———. *England of Charles II*. London: 1935.
Burnet (Bishop). *Burnet's History of His Own Time*. London: 1724.
Christie, W. D. *A Life of Anthony Ashley Cooper, First Earl of Shaftesbury*. London and New York: 1871.
Lingard, John. *A History of England*. London: 1829, 1831.
Ogg, David. *England in the Reign of Charles II*. London: 1934.
Pepys, Samuel. *The Diary of Samuel Pepys, Esq., F.R.S.* Edited by Richard Lord Braybrook. London: 1825.
Pollock, John. *The Popish Plot*. London: 1903.
Traill, H. D. *Shaftesbury*. New York: 1886.

QUEEN'S RIVAL, LOVER'S WIFE
The Scandalous Death of Amy Robsart

Kenilworth is a prime example of the fiction fact is stranger than. Amy Robsart was never a prisoner anywhere—certainly not in the castle of the title, which didn't belong to her husband, the Earl of Leicester, until some ten years after her death. Yet this novel by Sir Walter Scott is to be read and enjoyed for the sheer romance of it; the story was probably inspired by William Mickle's old Scottish ballad, reproduced in part at the beginning of this chapter. More authentic sources include an article by Lord Latymer in *Blackwood's Magazine* (New York and Edinburgh, March, 1932), entitled "The Mystery of Amy Robsart," as well as several booklets:

Frere, Sir Bartle Henry Temple. *Amy Robsart of Wymondham*. London: 1937.
Harris, Arthur. *Romance and Reality of Amy Robsart*. London: 192?.
Tighe, Hugh Usher. *An Historical Account of Cumner*. London: 1821.

The Harris piece, in fact, was written as the handbook for visitors to Kenilworth Castle. Two interesting and recently published works touch on the case and go into some detail concerning the private lives and loves of its principals. These are *Elizabeth and Leicester* (London, 1961) by Elizabeth Jenkins and *The Queens and the Hive* (London, 1962) by Dame Edith Sitwell. Andrew Lang's version of the case appears in *The Valet's Tragedy* (London, New York, and Bombay, 1903).

YOURS TRULY, JACK THE RIPPER
The Scourge of London's East End

Catherine Eddows' premonitory plaint is quoted from an episode in Tom Cullen's history of the Ripper murders, *When London Walked in Terror* (London, 1965). The book is strongly suggested for further reading. It is surely as complete and readable an account as one could ask. A useful companion volume would be *Jack the Ripper in Fact and Fiction* (London, 1965) by Robin Odell, which offers an anthology of prose reflecting the intrigue and the horror of that episode. Other readings include:

Anderson, Sir Robert. *The Lighter Side of My Official Life.* London: 1910.
Barnard, Allan. *The Harlot Killer.* New York, 1953.
McCormick, Donald. *The Identity of Jack the Ripper.* London: 1959.
Macnaghten, Sir Melville. *Days of My Years.* London: 1915.
Matters, Leonard. *The Mystery of Jack the Ripper.* London: 1928.
Stewart, William. *Jack the Ripper—A New Theory.* London: 1939.

GRAND DISGUISE
The Man in the Iron Mask

Chronicles of seventeenth-century France depict the splendor of the age. A few of the more useful here are:

Buranelli, Vincent. *Louis XIV.* New York: 1966.
Cronin, Vincent. *Louis Quatorzième.* Boston: 1965.
Lewis, W. H. *The Splendid Century.* New York: 1953.
Mitford, Nancy. *The Sun King.* New York: 1966.
Treasure, G. R. R. *Seventeenth Century France.* New York: 1966.
Voltaire. *The Age of Louis XIV.* Translated by Martyn P. Pollack. London: 1961.
Ziegler, Gilette. *At the Court of Versailles.* New York: 1966.

The perspective provides an interesting contrast to that of English accounts used for inquiry into the murder of Sir Edmund Godfrey and contemporary relations between Charles of England and Louis of France. Books dealing specifically with the Mask are *Man of the Mask* (London, 1908) by Arthur Stapylton Barnes and *The Man Behind the Mask* (London, 1954) by Rupert Furneaux. Andrew Lang examined the mystery at length in his *The Valet's Tragedy* (New York, London, and Bombay, 1903), which takes its title from this particular study. Hugh Ross Williamson's interview with Lord Quickwood is reported and developed in detail in his *Enigmas of History* (London, 1957). And, of course, the master storyteller's tale is available as

The Man in the Iron Mask, one segment of Alexandre Dumas' long romance, *Le Vicomte de Bragelonne,* first published during the late 1840s.

LOST DAUPHIN
The Unknown Fate of Louis XVII

Williams' claim to the title of Louis XVII is well presented by:

Evans, Elizabeth E. *The Story of Louis XVII of France.* London: 1893.
Hanson, John. *The Lost Prince.* New York: 1854.
Vinton, Francis. *Louis XVII and Eleazar Williams.* New York: 1868.

Miss Evans, however, devotes the better part of her work to a denial of Naundorff's claim rather than to her ostensible aim of supporting the Williams case. Naundorff, for his part, took the trouble to state his own case fully. His memoirs are published in English as the *Abridged Account of the Misfortune of the Dauphin* (London, 1898; translation by C. G. Perceval). Extracts appear also in *The King Who Never Reigned* (New York, 1909), which combines Naundorff's writings with Jean Eckard's *Memoirs Upon Louis XVII.* The memoirs of the dauphin's sister, Marie Thérése, appear with Jean Baptiste Harmand's reports on the prisoner in *Royal Memoirs on the French Revolution* (London, 1823). Sources indicating the possible truth of Naundorff's claim include Hans Roger Madol's *The Shadow King* (London, 1930). Audubon's case rests largely on Alice Jaynes Tyler's brief *I Who Should Command All* (New Haven, 1937). Other general references are:

Allen, Phoebe. *The Last Legitimate King of France, Louis XVII.* New York: 1912.
De Beauchesne, Alcide Hyacinthe Du Bois. *Louis XVII: His Life, His Suffering, His Death.* Translated by W. Hazlitt. New York: 1853.
Gosselin, Louis. *The Dauphin.*
Minnigerode, Meade. *The Son of Marie Antoinette.* New York: 1934.
Welch, Catherine. *The Little Dauphin.* New York: 1908.

LAST OF THE ROMANOVS
The Legend of Grand Duchess Anastasia

Many of the cited quotations were derived from commentary by Roland Krug von Nidda in an English translation of the autobiography

Ich Anastasia (London, New York, 1958) by Oliver Coburn. The recollections of Olga Alexandra are set forth in Ian Vorres' *The Last Grand Duchess* (New York, 1964). Other accounts related to the mystery of Anastasia's fate, mostly personal but often written to pass as historical, are found in:

Botkin, Gleb. *The Real Romanovs*. London, New York: 1931.
———. *The Woman Who Rose Again*. London, New York: 1937.
Buchanan, Sir George. *My Mission to Moscow*. New York, London: 1923.
Bykov, P. M. *The Last Days of Tsar Nicholas*. Translated with a preface by Andrew Rothstein. New York, London: 1934.
Rathlef-Keilmann, Harriet von. *Anastasia, Survivor of Ekaterinburg*. Translated by F. S. Flint. New York, London: 1928.
Vyrubova, Anna. *Memories of the Russian Court*. New York: 1923.

CROATOAN
The Lost Colony of Roanoke Island

Two collections of primary sources are recommended for further research into events surrounding the settling and disappearance of the Roanoke colony. One is *The Roanoke Voyages 1584-1590* (London, 1953, 1955), a two-volume, 1,000-page compilation of letters, notices, and other writings of the period, edited with narrative by David B. Quinn for the Hakluyt Society. Professor Quinn, a historian at the University College of Swansea (University of Wales) had previously made available a history of early English settlement in *Raleigh and the British Empire* (London, 1947), of which one chapter deals with the fate of those settlers at Roanoke Island. A North Carolina historian, Hugh T. Lefler, has edited another collection of documents called *North Carolina History Told By Contemporaries* (Chapel Hill, 1934), which includes the Lawson passage cited here. In addition, Professor Lefler has provided a concise and most interesting summary of that history in *The North Carolina Guide* (Chapel Hill, 1955), edited by Blackwell P. Robbins. Other histories worth noting in this context are:

Ashe, Samuel A'Court. *History of North Carolina*. Greensboro: 1908.
Hawks, Francis L. *History of North Carolina*. Fayetteville: 1857.
Stick, David. *The Outer Banks of North Carolina*. Chapel Hill: 1958.

THE CASE OF THE EMPTY COFFIN
Czar Alexander's Mysterious "Death"

Many histories of Russia touch on the curious death and possible disappearance of Czar Alexander I. Among the more rewarding are:

Clarkson, Jesse D. *A History of Russia.* New York: 1961.
Freeborn, Richard. *A Short History of Modern Russia.* New York: 1966.
Pares, Sir Bernard. *History of Russia.* New York, 1953.
Wren, Melvin C. *The Course of Russian History.* New York: 1963.

The subject is covered at greater length by:

Almedingen, E. M. *The Emperor Alexander I.* London: 1964.
Gribble, Francis. *Emperor and Mystic: The Life of Alexander I of Russia.* New York: 1931.
Lloyd, H. E. *Alexander I.* London: 1826.
Paleologue, Maurice. *The Enigmatic Czar.* New York, London: 1938.
Strakhovsky, L. I. *Alexander I of Russia.* New York: 1947.

The Grand Duke Nicholas, shortly before the end of the Romanov dynasty, compiled and edited Alexander's correspondence. It was published under the title, *Scenes of Russian Court Life* (London, no date given; translation by Henry Havelock).

FILE NO. 13595
The Disappearance of Judge Joseph Crater

The late Stella Crater, widow of the vanished judge, published (with Oscar Fraley) a personal account of her husband's life and career, *The Empty Robe* (New York, 1961); and that career allowed amply for the comfortable outlook of a loving wife. Plain faith in the man often begs to refute charges of moral or ethical misconduct unassisted; often it ignores the facts inherent in them. Crater's story, however, is in large measure the story of Tammany Hall in the early part of this century, and much of that story was disclosed by the famed Seabury investigations of the early 1930s. Those investigations may or may not have been directly related to Crater's demise, but they certainly touched on every aspect of his career up to that time. For accounts of these telling probes, see:

Chambers, Walter. *Samuel Seabury.* New York: 1932.
———. *Samuel Seabury: A Challenge.* New York: 1932.
Dewey, John. *New York and the Seabury Investigations.* New York: City Affairs Comm., 1933.
Northrup, William B. and John B. *The Insolence of Office.* New York: 1932.

Finally, of course, there is Seabury's *Final Report to the Joint Legislative Committee* in December, 1932.

FROM MU TO GONDWANALAND
The Mysterious Worlds of Prehistoric Man

The supercontinents hypothesis of Suess is proposed in *The Face of the Earth* (Oxford, 1904; translation by Hertha B. C. Sollas). Will Durant touches briefly on the various theories in *Our Oriental Heritage* (New York, 1954). Further adventures in the search to document such theories have recently been chronicled in *Saturday Review* by John Lear, science editor of the magazine.

TOWERS OF TOPAZ, TREES OF PEARL
The Lost Continent of Atlantis

Plato's writings in the *Timaeus* and *Critias* are drawn from *The Dialogues of Plato*, translated by Benjamin Jowett (New York, 1892). Other useful translations are:

Bury, Rev. R. G. *Plato*. Cambridge, Mass. and London: 1941.
Hamilton, Edith, and Cairns, Huntington. *The Dialogues of Plato*. New York: 1961.
Taylor, Thomas. *The Timaeus and Critias (of Atlanticus)*. New York: 1944.

Paul Friedlander's *Plato* (New York, 1958; translation by Hans Meyerhoff) is an especially valuable reference to the philosopher's geographic concept of Atlantis. The Aiken poem was originally published in *Priapus and the Pool and Other Poems* (New York, 1925). One of the best and most readily available books on the subject of lost continents in general—and Atlantis in particular—is Lyon Sprague de Camp's *Lost Continents* (New York, 1954). Other references include:

Bellamy, Hans Schindler. *The Atlantis Myth*. London: 1948.
Bramwell, James. *Lost Atlantis*. New York and London: 1938.
Saurat, Denis. *Atlantis and the Giants*. London: n.d.

James Mavor's speculations on the history and fate of Atlantis stem from the Aegean expedition he led in 1966. They are fully reported in his *Voyage to Atlantis* (New York, 1969). Nowhere, however, has the historic case for Atlantis been harder pressed than in the works of Ignatius Donnelly. A Minnesota lawyer and congressman by profession, Donnelly was a champion of agrarian reform movements toward the end of the nineteenth century. His spare time he devoted to a penetrating study of ancient history and the classics. He was fascinated with Atlantean legends and spent many hours each week poring over source materials in the Library of Congress. Shortly after his retirement from politics, he published his findings in a volume that remains today one of the most comprehensive ever to treat the subject, *Atlantis: The Antediluvian World* (New York, 1882; revised edition by Egerton Sykes, New York, 1949).

WHO DISCOVERED AMERICA?
Ancient Civilizations of the "New World"

Especially useful studies of the traditions of the biblical period are found in Sir James Frazer's *Folklore in the Old Testament* (London, 1919), Cyrus H. Gordon's *The Ancient Near East* (New York, 1953), William L. Wardle's *Israel and Babylon* (London, 1925) and his *Encyclopaedia Britannica* essay on the deluge, and a series of lectures by Dr. David Neiman at the New School for Social Research, New York, in 1966. Francisco López de Gómara's writings appear in *The Decades of the New World of West India* (London, 1555; translation by Richard Eden). Excerpts from writings by Prutz appear in de Camp (*op. cit.*). The renowned Sir Francis Bacon used the Atlantis-in-America theory for a novel he was never able to complete, *The New Atlantis*.

DANCE OF THE GIANTS
The Mystery of the Stonehenge Ruins

Gerald S. Hawkins' *Stonehenge Decoded* (New York, 1965) is *the* book for seekers after the truth of Stonehenge. It was written in collaboration with John B. White, an editor for the Smithsonian Astrophysical Observatory. Hawkins himself was a professor of astronomy at Boston University and a research associate at the Harvard College Observatory. Together they have come up with a work that is at once entertaining and enlightening. The book, which ends with a study of recent computer investigations of the monument's configuration, draws on works as far back as the medieval *History of the Kings of Britain* (London, 1966; translation by Lewis Thorpe) by Geoffrey of Monmouth. Among these, of course, the studies of R. J. C. Atkinson are most prominent. Atkinson, professor of archeology at University College, Cardiff, directed much of the recent digging about Stonehenge. His findings and his review of other sources are represented in *Stonehenge* (London, 1956), *Stonehenge and Avebury* (London, 1959), and an entry on the subject in the *Encyclopaedia Britannica*. The 1959 work was published by Her Majesty's Stationery Office as one of two guidebooks to the site; the other is *Stonehenge* (London, 1957) by R. S. Newall. Julius Caesar's classic report on Druid customs is taken from *The Gallic War and Other Writings*, translated by Moses Hadas (New York, 1957). Biographical information on John Aubrey is presented in detail by Oliver Lawson Dick in the introduction to his edition of Aubrey's *Brief Lives* (Ann Arbor, 1957).

YETI
The Legend of the Abominable Snowman

The story of the 1960-61 Himalayas expedition to discover the *Yeti* is excitingly told by Sir Edmund Hillary, leader of the party, and journalist Desmond Doig, in *High in the Thin, Cold Air* (Garden City, 1962). Hillary's Everest climb in 1953 is chronicled in his own *High Adventure* (New York, 1955) and in Sir John Hunt's *The Conquest of Everest* (New York, 1954), which includes a chapter by Hillary. Tensing Norkay, the Sherpa guide who has accompanied virtually all the major Himalayan adventures of recent decades, relates his life story and the story of those climbs in *Tiger of the Snows* (New York, 1955). The book includes native tales of the *Yeti*, including his father's own alleged eyewitness report. Studies of the *Yeti* legend are presented by Ralph Izzard in *The Abominable Snowman* (Garden City, 1955) and *An Innocent on Everest* (New York, 1954) and Ivan T. Sanderson in *Abominable Snowmen* (New York, Philadelphia, and London: 1961).

HIGHLAND FLING
The Search for the Loch Ness Monster

Tim Dinsdale's *Loch Ness Monster* (London, 1961) offers a good review of details that have accumulated over the years—over the millennia, in fact, beginning with the admonition of Saint Columba in A.D. 565. Earlier investigations by Rupert T. Gould into the mystery were presented in his *The Loch Ness Monster and Others* (London, 1934); the highly regarded English commander had previously published *The Case for the Sea Serpent* (London, 1930). However, contemporary newspaper accounts still provide the most exciting view of the case, involving as they do the day-by-day unfolding of its many facets.

Index

A

Abominable Snowman (*Yeti*), 192–199
Aiken, Conrad, 164, 165
Albertina (aircraft), 17, 20, 22, 23, 28
  crash investigation, 24
  as Transair property, 26
Aldabra Island, 161
Alexander I, Czar
  as "Alexander the Blessed," 129
  becomes interested in religion, 131
  brother Constantine, 135, 136
  brother Grand Duke Michael, 138
  brother Nicholas to succeed him, 132
  death, 134, 135
  efforts to make peace with Napoleon, 130
  father Paul I, 128, 129, 139
  goes to Taganrog, 132
  as hermit in Siberia, 136, 137–139
  Holy Alliance Covenant, 131
  peak of his prestige, 130, 131
  wife Alexandra, 132
Alexander II, 137
Alexander III, 137
Allen-Julien dialogue, 25
Alport, Lord, 22, 23
Anderson, Robert, 67, 70, 71
Anne of Austria, 81
Anne, Queen (France), 77, 85, 86
Antoinette, Marie, 78, 90, 91
Appleyard, John, 55
Aquila, Bishop of, 52
Argentina, 160
Arlington, Lord, 84
Atkins, Samuel, 39
Atkinson, R. J. C., 184–185
Atlantis, 161, 164, 167–169, 177
  as "Lost Continent," 174
  in Plato writings, *Critias*, 165, 166
  in Plato writings, *Republic*, 166
  in Plato writings, *Timaeus*, 165, 166

Aubrey, John, 181
  Brief Lives, 181–183, 186
Audubon, John J., 95, 96, 98
Australia, 160

B

Barnes, Monsignor A. S., 83, 84
Barnett, Reverend Samuel, 63
Beaker people, 183
Beaufort, Duc de, 76, 80, 81
Bedloe, William, 39
Beebe, Dr. William, 206
Bellasis, Lord, 39, 41
Benningsen (Hanoverian general), 128, 129
Bernadotte, Count Folke, 20
Berner Street (London), 65
Berry, Henry, 40, 42
Billy Haas Restaurant, 146
Blair, Reverend David H., 205
Bloom, Murray T., 152
Blount, Thomas, 53, 55
Bonaparte, Napoleon, 77, 130
Botkin, Gleb, 114
Botkin, Dr. Eugene, 106
Buck's Row (London), 62
Buffon, 164
Burnet, Gilbert, 37
Bury, Howard, 192
Buxhoeveden, Baroness Isa, 107

C

Caesar, Julius, 182
Camp, Lyon S., de, 158, 159
  Lost Continents, 175
Capet, Louis Charles, 90–94, 96
Carr, John D., 45
Castlereagh, Lord, 131
Catherine, Queen, 34
Catholics, treatment in days of King Charles II, 34
Cayuga Democratic Club, 144
Cecilie, Crown Princess, 109
Chapman, "Dark Annie," 63, 66, 67
Chapman, George, 72
Charles II, King, 32, 41, 43, 76, 82–84, 181
  purported plots against, 33, 34
  restrictions, prejudices against Catholics, 34